WOODWORKING PLANES

A

Descriptive Register

of

Wooden Planes

By ALVIN SELLENS

PRIVATELY PRINTED

Library of Congress Catalog

Card Number 78-52687

Available from
Alvin Sellens
134 Clark St.
Augusta, Ks. 67010

Table of Contents

Preface

This volume is intended to be a descriptive compilation of the basic information known about the many varieties of wooden woodworking planes used in America. It is hoped that this compilation will stimulate interest in the collecting and preservation of wooden tools. Many scarce planes are doubtlessly rusting and rotting away in unused tool boxes and sheds throughout the country but lack of proper identification hampers their discovery and preservation. Emphasis here-in is placed on identification, description and proper name of each variety of wooden plane. Names of the planes are considered to be of primary importance inasmuch as names are the basis for all communication on the subject. Without a common baseline of terminology, everything from research to swap-shopping is needlessly inhibited. The scope of this book is generally limited to those planes made by American planemakers on a commercial basis. Most of the information was drawn from the best of all possible sources; that is, the data published by the actual makers and sellers in the form of catalogs and sales sheets. Backup material was drawn from a variety of written sources, personal observation and numerous contacts with knowledgeable students and collectors.

It is recognized that many varieties of planes are not mentioned in this book. Numerous entries in the makers' catalogs are not sufficiently illustrated to warrant positive identification. In other cases, some planes noted in collections have not been associated with a catalog name.

A reference number has been assigned each plane for ease of discussion and indexing. The grouping and numbering system is strictly arbitrary and is not intended to imply that the plane makers or users thought of them in this manner. The first digit of the number refers to a general type such as a bench plane or rabbeting plane. The alphabetic designation refers to a group of planes such as smooth planes or filletsters within the general type. The last digit or digits is a numerical listing of the varieties of planes within the group such as the several varieties of smooth planes.

Supportable data and illustrations on additional planes would be welcomed by the author. Constructive criticism of any nature will be duly noted and filed in the hope that a future edition can be published that will include additional information.

Acknowledgments

The author gratefully acknowledges assistance and/or data provided by:

William J. Baader	Springfield, Ohio
Fred H. Bair	Auburndale, Florida
Norman Benson	Marlow, Oklahoma
Carl E. Bopp	Audubon, New Jersey
Connecticut Historical Soc.	Hartford, Connecticut
William Evans	Mogadore, Ohio
W. L. Gordon	Bull Shoals, Arkansas
Robert D. Graham, Jr.	Sacramento, California
William P. Graves	Springfield, Ohio
Marion Henley	Columbia, Missouri
Russell A. Herner	Bellevue, Ohio
H. A. Hinz	Clinton, Oklahoma
Herman Maddocks	Massachusetts
Ohio Historical Soc. Museum	Columbus, Ohio
William R. Rigler	Northbrook, Illinois
Ivan C. Risley	Kansas City, Missouri
Elliot M. Sayward	Levittown, New York
Alexa Sellens	Augusta, Kansas
David A. Sellens	Wichita, Kansas
Geraldine M. Sellens	Augusta, Kansas
Roger K. Smith	Lancaster, Massachusetts
Mark A. Sutterby	Udall, Kansas
Raymond R. Townsend	Williamsburg, Virginia
Max R. Tully	Wichita, Kansas
George D. Tuttle	Columbus, Ohio
Anne Wing	Marion, Massachusetts
Donald B. Wing	Marion, Massachusetts

Wooden Planes

The basic definition of a plane in a woodworking sense could be stated as "A holding fixture for obtaining depth control of a wood chisel." Probably the first plane was made by crudely attaching a sharp object to a plank thus controlling the depth of cut over an uneven surface. The hundreds of sizes, shapes, materials and adjustment features of planes are only adaptations of that chisel-holding concept.

The hand plane has been a widely used tool since the early Roman period. The many refinements and multitude of varieties are a clear indication of the importance of this type of tool. The Romans used metal bodied and metal shod planes as early as the fourth century but apparently the concept of metal planes was cast aside or lost for several centuries. Wood was the primary material used for making planes in the modern historical period up to the last quarter of the nineteenth century. The cast metal plane was patented in 1827 but it wasn't until the seventies that metal planes began to seriously compete with the well established wooden plane industry. The superiority of metal planes and the availability and variety of power driven wood working tools has slowed the wooden planemaking business to a trickle. Wooden planes are still available on the shelf in many parts of the world but are no longer made in the United States.

In all probability, the first woodworking plane made in America was whittled out by an immigrant carpenter or cooper to match the irons that he carried with him to the new world. It is also probable that these planes were identical to their predecessors that the craftsman had also made for his own use in England. As building and the building trades expanded in America, it was natural that the tools followed the styles of England inasmuch as both culture and trade were controlled by British law. It must be remembered that manufacturing in America was discouraged by the British prior to the Revolutionary War. England preferred to keep the colonies in the role of producers of raw material and as users of manufactured goods. Several 18th century American planemakers have been identified; however it is generally conceded that the bulk of the planes sold in America through the first quarter of the 19th century were imported from England. Planemaking, as a craft, proliferated in America during the second quarter of the 19th century and reached its apex during the third quarter. By 1900, the number of planemakers had dwindled to a mere handful of large companies producing a vast variety of different sizes, shapes and qualities of planes. Ohio Tool Company offered a complete line of wooden planes in their 1914 catalog (Ref. 5) and some of the wholesale catalogs offered them for several years after that date. It is doubtful that there were many buyers after World War I.

The American made wooden plane, whose roots were English, continued in the English style with unique features that can only be described as American. The most apparent American feature has been described as a look of utility or as having a slightly crude appearance when compared to a

7

similar item made in England in the same time period. The American plane will characteristically have less chamfer on the corners, slightly more depth in the body and will lack the fineness of material and workmanship seen in English planes. The early English moulding planes were often ¼ to ½ inch longer than American moulding planes. The upper portion of the tote on American planes is apt to have less backward projection than English planes. No one knows when or why these subtle differences began to appear but it is known that they appeared quite early in the American planemaking period. Planes made in the 1840s were definitely of this so-called American style. The blunter less-finished look of American planes is thought by some to be a result of the Yankee urge to do things faster and to emphasize quantity rather than detail fineness. It seems more likely that this approach had its beginning in the use of prison labor to make planes. Large quantities of planes were made by forced labor with little, if any, incentive to add the extra quality normally provided by a true craftsman. The influx of these cheaper prison-made planes on the market would have the tendency to force the other planemakers to market a competitive product.

In addition to the differences in appearance, the American planemaking industry developed minor differences in plane names and terminology. Examples of these differences are the American usage of the terms fore plane and leveling plane. It has also been noted that the names of several of the moulding planes are different when comparing American and British reference data of the same time period. Discussions of plane names are included under the various plane headings.

During the last quarter of the 19th century, the planemaking industry was subjected to three massive influences. First there was the intense competition of the iron planes which were becoming cheaper and more versatile at an ever-increasing rate. The iron planes were generally conceded to be better and were certainly more positive in the area of adjustments. The second influence was the increasing availability of mill-cut mouldings and the wider variety of pre-finished wood products. The resulting decrease in handwork eliminated the need for many special types of planes. The last of these factors was the consolidation of the plane industry into the hands of a few large makers. The increasing use of large powered machinery hastened the demise of the small planemaking craft shops in much the same manner as small operators continue to disappear in every industry.

From the vantage point of almost a century later it is easy to see that the end of the wooden plane industry was inevitable and that there was little that could be done to delay its demise. The large companies apparently interpreted the decrease in sales as a need to provide a wider variety of planes. The plane buyer of 1900 must have been overwhelmed by the choice of wooden, wood bottom and metal planes available on the shelf. For instance, Ohio Tool Company listed no less than 41 different smoothing planes in their 1901 catalog. Despite these last-ditch efforts, the wooden planemaking business in America essentially ceased about 1925.

Types of Wood

Most of the American wooden planes are made of beechwood variously described as straight grained, second growth and white beech. Some early American planes are made of white and yellow birch but most of the catalogs mention beech as being the standard material for planes. The use of birch for plane making was apparently discontinued prior to the general usage of catalogs as a means of advertising planes. British planes were also generally made of beechwood; however, English beech is quite different from American beech. One of the earliest Roman planes known is also made partially of beechwood. Beech was used because of its density, toughness and resistance to warping. American beech is a straight grained white to light tan wood characterized by cross grained flecks. Oils and age in combination with handling results in a golden tan appearance. Other hardwoods such as apple were used to a lesser degree; however, applewood planes are considerably more scarce because of their higher original cost. In some cases a combination of beech with a more expensive wood was used such as a beechwood panel plow with apple or boxwood arms. An occasional maple plane is seen and maple was frequently used for the top boards of the coopers howels and crozes. For those who wanted better quality; boxwood, rosewood and ebony planes of certain types were available at prices considerably higher than the beechwood planes. In other parts of the world, woods such as teak, ironwood and hornbeam were used and occasionally one of these planes is seen in the United States. Oak, walnut and even hickory were used for homemade planes.

Many planes have facings on the sole or have inserts at projecting rub points and corners to reduce wearing and thus increase the useful life of the tool. These wear strips were usually made of Turkey boxwood which is one of the hardest of woods. Planes fitted with such wear strips were said to be boxed, single boxed, double boxed, boxed faced, etc. to generally describe the boxwood application. In some cases the boxwood inserts were dovetailed into the plane body but in many cases the strips were inserted into grooves with only the friction of a close tolerance fit to hold them in place. Ebony and lignum vitae were also used occasionally for wear strips.

The finish on wooden planes was generally a thin coating of oil. Some of the better quality planes were finished with clear shellac or varnish. Inasmuch as the finish quickly wore off at the rub points, the varnished or shellacked planes are more apt to have a varied color when restored.

Most suppliers made only passing reference to the woods used for planemaking. Inasmuch as the tools were being sold to the woodworking trades, the wooden parts would speak for themselves. It was therefore gratifying that Hynson's Tool and Supply Company catalog (Ref. 38) devoted an entire page to the woods used in tool making. Although this supplier specialized in coopers tools, the comments are considered to be generally applicable to all wooden planes. The entire page is quoted.

WOOD.

Few people realize that the selection of Timber suitable for the purpose of manufacturing tools of is often a very difficult matter and requires great care in the selection of the same. The wood suitable for the manufacture of coopers' tools must be a wood that is close-grained and of a hard texture so as to resist as much as possible the wear of wood against wood in the use of the same. The wood must be thoroughly dry, and dried in such a manner that under ordinary conditions there will be no warpage of the same while in use. Following we give a brief description of the various kinds of woods we have found suitable for the manufacture of Cooperage Tools and Hoops.

APPLEWOOD.

The Applewood used by us is from sound stock, and the largest portion of the same we get from New York state and Ohio. The Ohio Applewood is of a dark red color and very even grained; while the New York wood is of a lighter color, but of as close a grain as that from Ohio. We use Applewood in the manufacture of Croze Boards, Jointers, Levelers and Bung Starters, as it has but few equals for the purpose.

BEECH.

Beech wood we obtain from various localities, and we find that it varies but little. Eastern wood is of a light brown nut color, while the western stock is of a lighter color, but of same texture and hardness. We use Beech wood for Croze Boards, Jointers and Levelers, while the same is not as well suited for this purpose as Applewood. Still it is a very serviceable wood and lower in price.

CHERRY.

We use Cherry wood only as a filler or for blocking up on tools, and never where there is any wear to the same.

GUAN DE PINON.

Better known as Pinon wood. This is a new wood that we import from Cuba, is of a reddish brown, color resembling walnut somewhat; is of a close grain and heavy in weight. Takes a fine polish. We use this wood for Croze Boards only and send it out only upon order for same. Ask us for a sample when ordering goods of us. We will be pleased to send it.

HICKORY.

Hickory wood is too well known to need a description of the same. We use only second growth Hickory, and make from the same Tress Hoops, Drivers' Handles and Frames.

LIGNUM VITAE.

Lignum Vitae has become well known to the cooperage trade. It is a wood of an oily nature, close grained and heavy. We import this wood from Mexico, Peru and Chili. The Mexican wood is dark in color. The Peru wood varies in color from a light greenish yellow to a dark green, and is the best wood we receive. The wood from Chili is of a light brown color to a dark brown, and is very oily. We use Lignum Vitae for Croze Runners, Levelers, Croze Boards and on faces of all crozing tools where there is a great deal of wear.

MAPLE.

The Maple we use is of the hard white variety and Bird's Eye Maple, used in making Croze Boards and Jointers only.

SANGRE DE TORO.

This is a wood native to Cuba and the Philippines and is the hardest wood we have. There is, in fact, no grain to the same. It is of a light yellow color and heavier in weight than Lignum Vitae. It is not possible for us to put a fine finish to this wood, as the grain and hardness of the same will not permit it. We use this wood for Croze Boards and Runners, and send it out only when called for.

By specifying any of the above woods when ordering from us we will furnish the same.

Markings

The maker's name normally appears on the front or toe end of the wooden plane. Quite often the maker's stamp included the city or city and state and occasionally the complete address. It is not uncommon for the maker's mark to be inclosed within a serrated or scalloped border. These marks were normally placed in a symmetrical position on the tool in contrast with the owners stamp which was quite often placed with less care. The owners stamp was also apt to be imprinted on the toe but might also be applied on any or all sides. This stamp was primarily an identification for ownership purposes and was therefore commonly applied in more than one place on the plane in order to be readily seen. The marks of more than one owner on a plane are an indication of age inasmuch as personal tools were generally sold or passed down only at death or retirement of the owner.

The mark of a dealer or jobber is also occasionally noted on a wooden plane. A dealer sometimes used a symbol such as a star or square applied to the toe end of the plane as a method of identification of items sold through his shop. The larger jobbers such as E.C. Simmons had complete lines of planes made with their brand name applied; however, most of these planes did not include a maker's name or mark. Some of the larger makers made more than one quality of planes and marked the second rate items with a brand name rather than the company name. A good example of this is the Scioto planes which are actually second grade tools made by Ohio Tool Company.

The numbers on the heel of a wooden plane are either type numbers or sizes or both. Sizes numbers are specified in inches with the exception of hollows and rounds which are discussed elsewhere. These numbers were placed on the heel to allow quick selection of particular plane from the set as they rested on the shelf or tool box tray. The methods of specifying sizes are discussed under the various plane headings. The type numbers are the manufacturers' designation of a given variety of plane. These numbers were no doubt useful in ordering, stocking and billing as well as in advertising. It can easily be seen why a company like Ohio Tool needed a numbering system when it is realized that several hundred planes were offered in a single catalog. Type numbers are extremely valuable to the collector in that they provide positive correlation between a catalog listing and an actual plane. It is unfortunate that only a few of the large makers used type numbering on their tools. A cross reference of some of the more common numbers is included elsewhere in this volume.

Plane Irons

The word "iron" refers to the cutting blade of the plane and is a carryover from the early days when the cutter was the only metal used in plane manufacture. The word is still used in this context even for modern planes made entirely of metal. Irons were also called bits by some wooden plane makers. The word "iron" is also used to designate the chip breaker or cap iron which is fastened to the cutting iron to form the so-called double iron. Double irons came into use in the last half of the eighteenth century, however, both single and double iron bench planes were sold throughout the nineteenth century. Double iron planes became far more popular than the single varieties and as a result, single iron bench planes are relatively scarce.

The top iron is positioned about 1/16 of an inch back of the cutting edge on bench planes and acts to break the chips quickly thus avoiding the tendency of the wood to split ahead of the cutting edge. Irons of the wood-bodied planes tapered with the thickest portion close to the cutting edge. These thick irons were rigid and therefore resisted chattering. Use of a cap iron also increased rigidity and resistance to chattering. The words "cast steel" were imprinted on many plane irons and was considered a mark of quality. This terminology originally referred to special small batch preparation of high quality carbon steel as compared to the softer wrought varieties but later became merely an indication that the item was made of good cutting steel.

Many of the older irons and practically all of the moulding plane irons were made of two pieces of metal hammered together such that only the cutting edge was made of high quality steel. This joint is visible on many irons from wooden planes. A well made plane body would often outlast the iron and as a result many of the older planes have replacement irons installed. In addition, many of the early American made planes had English irons installed when new. For these reasons, estimations of the age and origin of a plane should not be based upon the markings of the iron.

Bench plane irons were usually bedded at approximately 45 degrees as discussed elsewhere and moulding plane irons were set several degrees higher. This comparatively steep set was satisfactory on moulding planes because moulding cuts were always made with the grain and only the best straight grained lumber was used. Bench plane irons were listed in practically every catalog but replacement irons for moulding planes were seldom listed. Irons were rarely replaced in moulding planes because of the difficulty in grinding a blank to the proper contour.

Bench Planes

Numerical listing of bench planes.

Ref. No.	NAME
1A1	Smooth Plane
1A2	Smooth Plane, Solid Handle
1A3	Smooth Plane, Jack Handle
1A4	Smooth Plane, German Pattern
1A5	Smooth Plane, Front Knob
1A6	Smooth Plane, Handled, Front Knob
1A7	Smooth Plane, Double Razee
1A8	Smooth Plane, Carriage Makers'
1A9	Smooth Plane, Ship
1A10	Smooth Plane, Boys
1A11	Smooth Plane, Heald Patent
1A12	Smooth Plane, Palmers' Patent
1A13	Smooth Plane, Bailey Patent
1A14	Smooth Plane, Adjustable Throat
1A15	Smooth Plane, Double Wedge
1A16	Smooth Plane, Tabor Patent
1B1	Jack Plane
1B2	Jack Plane, Razee
1B3	Jack Plane, German Pattern
1B4	Jack Plane, Double Razee
1B5	Jack Plane, Front Knob
1B6	Jack Plane, Ship
1C1	Fore Plane
1C2	Fore Plane, Razee
1C3	Fore Plane, Double Razee
1C4	Fore Plane, Front Knob
1C5	Fore Plane, Ship
1C6	Fore Plane, Rust Patent
1C7	Fore Plane, Double Wedge
1D1	Jointer Plane
1D2	Jointer Plane, Razee
1D3	Jointer Plane, Double Razee
1D4	Jointer Plane, Front Knob
1D5	Jointer Plane, Lightweight
1D6	Jointer Plane, Ship

Bench Planes

The family of flat-soled planes made for smoothing a workpiece is called Bench planes. These planes were used to smooth the surfaces of the boards that were received from the sawyer with all four sides rough. In ascending order of size, the smooth, jack, fore and jointer comprise this category. In addition to the flat sole, all bench planes have the common characteristic of a closed throat with a center cavity for upward discharge of shavings. Bench plane irons are generally set at 45 degrees from horizontal which is called common pitch. The many American manufacturers were quite consistent in the iron angle and in the wide square-cut mouth opening. The mouth opening in the upper surface of American-made planes is characteristically as large as possible for the sake of utility as opposed to many European planes with ornamental or sharply tapered mouths.

American manufacturers were also fairly consistent in names and terminology versus the various sizes of planes. In fact, the makers were far more consistent than most of the relevant literature including the prose of many modern writers. For instance, some writers still insist upon discussing Try or Trying planes in connection with American tools without realizing that these are primarily European terms. Many references to Trying planes do exist in early American writings and inventories because of English influence and English imports; however, the maker's catalogs and listings included Jack and Fore planes almost without exception. Philip Chapin of Baltimore and V.A. Emond & Co. (Ref. 33) of Quebec are the only two American makers known to have listed Trying planes. The Emond catalog referred to "Trying or Fore" planes. The Strike Block, Long plane and Intermediate Smooth plane are other terms somewhat carelessly applied to American bench planes by persons other than plane makers. Without further belaboring the point, the Smooth, Jack, Fore and Jointer planes comprise the full complement of American bench planes.

Most varieties of bench planes were available with either single or double irons. Those equipped with double irons were slightly more expensive than the single-iron types but were evidently far more popular judging from the relative scarcity of single-iron planes. The irons were held in place by wooden wedges. The wedge was called an Iron Holder by one maker.

The round button on the upper surface of many of the larger planes and on the heel of most smooth planes was called a Start or a Start Pin by the plane suppliers. Striking the start a sharp blow with a mallet while grasping the wedge served to easily loosen the wedge and iron. The start was made of a hard material, usually a dense end-grain piece of wood, and was rounded off to avoid splintering on the edges. The rarer hardwoods were sometimes used on the more expensive planes and even metal was occasionally provided. Bench planes were listed by various makers with starts described as wood, boxwood, polished wood, ebony, lignum vitae, polished iron, steel and silver mounted. One reference referred to the start as a Strike Button.

Bench planes with the tote set low on a cutaway section of the plane body are called Razee planes. Many suppliers offered razee planes but usually priced them slightly higher than the corresponding square type, which probably accounts for their relative scarcity. It has been noted that some modern writers and collectors refer to all Razee planes as Ship planes. Such is not the case. Several catalogs covered two complete listings of Razee planes, one group was called Carpenters Razee or just Razee while the other listing was referred to as Ship planes. The Ship planes were invariably listed only in narrow widths. It is concluded that all Ship planes are razee but all Razee planes are not Ship. A comparison of widths shown under the individual headings will point up the difference between a Carpenters Razee plane and a Ship plane.

The more expensive bench planes had additional features listed such as bolted handles, brass nuts to fasten the irons together, and varnished or polished bodies. Some suppliers also listed various optional irons such as American, English or American Best. One supplier even listed bench planes without irons.

A review of the plane iron listings of the major makers casts only slight additional information on the subject of bench planes. Both single and double bench plane irons were listed by several suppliers in sizes of 1½ to 3 inches which is essentially the complete size span of smooth to jointer planes. Bench plane irons were always listed as a group and not as irons for smooth, jack, etc. This would certainly imply that all new irons were ground the same when initially delivered. It is also noted that none of the trade literature mentioned curvature of irons in connection with their description of the different sizes and types of planes. Much has been written about the differences in the shape of a jack plane iron and those of other planes such as a jointer. A most concise definition is included in *Audels Carpenters and Builders Guide (Ref. 23)* which includes sketches of the various irons. The general theory that a jack plane iron is ground slightly convex for easy cutting of rough work is undoubtedly correct and will not be debated. However, it is reasonable to assume that the irons in new bench planes were ground flat when new and it therefore follows that curvature of the iron was generally determined by the owner. This would account for the fact that many extant wooden jack planes are equipped with irons that are ground straight rather than convex.

Smooth Planes

Smooth planes or smoothing planes are the smallest members of the bench plane family. They range in length from 7 to 10½ inches except for some special varieties such as the carriage makers' smooth planes which are slightly shorter. The irons are generally 1½ to 2½ inches wide although both narrower and wider ones were made. Wider irons were available by special order at extra cost. These planes were used to make the final finish cuts on the surface of the workpiece. They were relatively short to allow cleanup around obstructions and on small surfaces.

The iron of a smooth plane is ground essentially straight across with only a slight curve at each edge to reduce tearing of the wood. It is shaped the same as for a jointer plane, however the smooth plane is too short to smooth a long workpiece for precision joining. The smooth and jack planes are the most numerous of all planes inasmuch as they were standard tool box items for the beginning carpenter as well as for the master specialists. The start, when used on a smooth plane, was generally on the heel of the plane body. On the handled smooth planes, it was located on the upper surface of the plane body forward of the iron.

Many smooth planes were available with an adjustable throat or mouth. This adjustment feature generally consisted of a fixed insert in the sole forward of the iron. The insert could be shortened or replaced with a longer one to widen or narrow the throat as desired. It could also be replaced when worn, thus increasing the life of the plane. Inasmuch as smooth planes were used primarily to make finish cuts, the throat was normally set narrow and the iron was set fine.

Except where noted on the individual descriptions, smooth planes were made from beechwood.

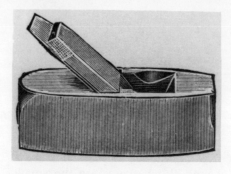

1914 (Ref. 5)

No. 1A1 Smooth Plane

1A1   SMOOTH PLANE
This standard pattern plane was listed in most catalogs merely as a smooth plane. When a catalog or price list included more than one pattern, this type was sometimes listed as an Oval Smooth or as a Common Smooth plane.
Length: 7¾ to 9 inches. A common length was 8 inches.
Iron Width: 1½ to 2½ inches. A common width was 2 inches.
Iron type: Single or double
Wood: Beech, apple, boxwood, rosewood or ebony
Additional features: Available with an adjustable mouth. This feature was also called a Slip Mouth.
This is the most common type of the smooth planes and probably the most common of all wooden planes. The tapered stock was a feature standardized in England and adopted by American planemakers. The stock is wider at the center to provide additional strength to hold the iron and still provide maneuverability in small areas. Planes of this pattern were made in America throughout the wooden plane era.

1914 (Ref. 5)

Right Handed Handle

No. 1A2 Smooth Plane, Solid Handle

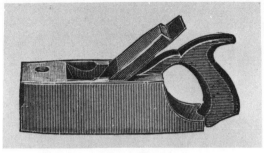

1901 (Ref. 1)

Round Handle

No. 1A2 Smooth Plane, Solid Handle

1A2   SMOOTH PLANE, SOLID HANDLE
The tapered shape sometimes resulted in these planes being listed as Oval Shaped or Oval. They were also listed as Razee or Recess Handle smooth planes. The handle and main body of the plane were generally made from a single piece of wood but an occasional item is seen in which the body and handle were made separately.
Length: 10¼ to 10½ inches. Length refers to the overall length of the tool including the handle.
Iron Width: 1⅞ to 2½ inches. A common width was 2 inches.
Iron Type   Single or double
Wood: Beech, apple, boxwood or rosewood
Additional Features: Available with an adjustable mouth which was also called a Slip Mouth. A choice of either a right handed or a round handle, as shown in the illustration, was offered by some suppliers.
Because of the higher original cost and the tendency toward breakage of the handle, planes of this type in good condition are quite scarce.

1908 (Ref. 4)

No. 1A3 Smooth Plane, Jack Handle

1A3   SMOOTH PLANE, JACK HANDLE
Also listed as a Smooth Plane with Applied Handle or Razee Smooth Plane with Jack Handle.
Length: 9½ inches approximately
Iron Width: 2 to 2¼ inches
Iron Type: Double
The CHIPAWAY name shown on the side of the illustrated plane was an E.C. Simmons Hardware Company trademark used on second quality planes.

21

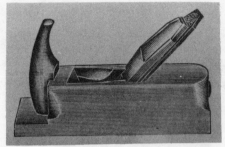

1914 (Ref. 5)

No. 1A4 Smooth Plane, German Pattern

1A4 SMOOTH PLANE, GERMAN PATTERN

Also listed as Smooth Plane with Horn, Bull Plane, or as a German Smooth Plane.

Length: 8¼ to 8½ inches
Iron Width: 1¼ to 2 inches
Iron Type: Single or double

These planes were offered with a choice of the irons being either square or rounded on the upper end. German pattern planes were offered in the United States over a long period but were never popular. American made planes of this type are scarce.

1908 (Ref. 4)

No. 1A5 Smooth Plane, Front Knob

1A5 SMOOTH PLANE, FRONT KNOB

This type plane was listed by Ohio Tool Company (Ref. 1) in 1901 under the heading of "Improved Wood Planes."

Length: 8 inches
Iron Width: 2 to 2¼ inches
Iron Type: Double

The plane shown in the illustration has a painted hardwood knob advertised as "Ebonized." A plain wood knob was also used on some Keen Kutter planes of this type. Keen Kutter was a trade mark of the Simmons Hardware Company of St. Louis, Missouri. The actual maker of Keen Kutter planes has not been determined; however, it is known that the Ohio Tool Company offered a line of planes almost identical to the plane shown in the illustration.

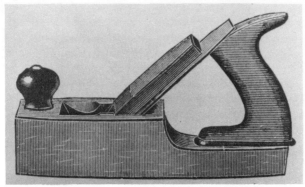

1914 (Ref. 5)

No. 1A6 Smooth Plane, Handled, Front Knob

1A6   SMOOTH PLANE, HANDLED, FRONT KNOB
Length: 9½ or 9⅝ inches
Iron Width: 2 to 2¼ inches
Iron Type: Double
The front knob on the illustrated plane was finished with a hard black paint and advertised as being "Ebonized." Planes of this type have been noted with Ohio Tool and Keen Kutter markings.

The rear tote is fastened to a metal plate with one through-bolt after the plate is secured to the plane body with wood screws.

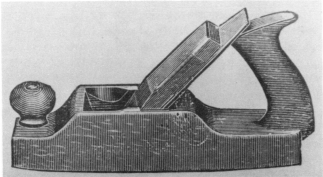

1914 (Ref. 5)

No. 1A7 Smooth Plane, Double Razee

1A7   SMOOTH PLANE, DOUBLE RAZEE
The term Double Razee is used for descriptive purposes only and was not used by the makers. This type of plane was listed by Ohio Tool Company (Ref. 1) in 1901 under the heading of "Improved Wood Planes."
Length: 10¼ inches
Iron Width: 2 or 2⅛ inches
Iron Type   Double

23

1880 (Ref. 15)

No. 1A8 Smooth Plane, Carriage Makers'

1A8   SMOOTH PLANE, CARRIAGE MAKERS'
Also listed as a Coach Makers' Smooth Plane.

These planes are essentially a shorter version of the common oval pattern smooth plane listed as No. 1A1.
Length: Approximately 6 inches
Iron Width: 1½ to 2 inches
Iron Type: Double

1872 (Ref. 18)

No. 1A9 Smooth Plane, Ship

1A9   SMOOTH PLANE, SHIP
The ship smooth plane is merely a narrower version of the oval pattern smooth. The overlap in sizes noted between various makers would indicate that a ship plane sold by one maker might be identical to a common narrow smooth plane sold by another supplier.
Length: 8 to 9 inches
Wood Type: Beech, rosewood or lignum vitae
Iron Width: 1½ to 2⅛ inches
Iron Type: Single or double

Sellens Collection

No. 1A10 Smooth Plane, Boys

1A10   SMOOTH PLANE, BOYS
The smooth planes made for boys tool boxes were scaled down versions of the common type smooth planes. They were both narrower and shorter than the common planes in order to fit the hands of a boy. Unlike the toy planes mentioned elsewhere, these planes were made to actually cut wood. Double irons were common and one supplier offered boys planes made of boxwood.

The illustrated plane is marked Keen Kutter. It is 5½ inches long and has a 1½ inch iron.

Roger K. Smith Collection

No. 1A11 Smooth Plane, Heald Patent

1A11   SMOOTH PLANE, HEALD PATENT
The iron holding mechanism of this plane was patented April 22, 1878 by Addison Heald who was a plane maker of Milford, New Hampshire.

No. 1A12 Smooth Plane, Palmers' Patent

1A12   SMOOTH PLANE, PALMERS' PATENT
   Length: 8 inches
   Iron Width: 2 inches
   The toe end of the illustrated plane is stamped Palmers' Patent, Pd Feb 3rd 1857 Auburn, N.Y. This patent is an early attempt to apply the adjustable iron principle to a wooden plane. Adjustment features were incorporated into most metal planes as early as the 1870's but such features were rarely applied to wooden planes. We can speculate that survival of wooden planes in competition with the metal counterparts depended largely upon the lower price of the wooden varieties. This same competition factor perhaps tended to keep the wooden planes as simple as possible.

No. 1A13 Smooth Plane, Bailey Patent

26

1A13   SMOOTH PLANE, BAILEY PATENT

The Leonard Bailey plane patents made famous by Stanley Rule & Level Company on iron planes were used on wooden smooth planes prior to sale of the patents to Stanley in 1869. The illustrated plane is marked C.E. Smith on the toe and a similar plane owned by Roger K. Smith is marked G.A. Benton. Use of these patents was probably licensed to plane makers in the area. Both of the planes mentioned carry the Bailey patent date on the lever cap. The adjustment lever shown below the iron is an up and down adjustment of the iron rather than the familiar lateral adjust feature which later used the same type of lever.

The lever cap feature has been noted on several wooden planes, however it is generally apparent that the cap was added by the owner rather than by the maker. Commercially manufactured planes of this variety are scarce.

Roger K. Smith Collection

No. 1A14 Smooth Plane, Adjustable Throat

1A14   SMOOTH PLANE, ADJUSTABLE THROAT

This standard sized smooth plane has a bottom shoe forward of the iron that can be moved forward thus widening the throat. The movable shoe is locked in place by tightening the large screw on top of the plane. The illustrated plane is of English manufacture and is marked Greenslade, Bristol.

George Tuttle Collection

No. 1A15 Smooth Plane, Double Wedge

27

1A15 SMOOTH PLANE, DOUBLE WEDGE
This standard sized smooth plane has two wedges. The bottom wedge is
fastened to the plane body with a screw through a slotted hole in the wedge.
Adjusting the wedges will result in varying the pitch of the iron and varying
the width of the mouth opening. The plane was made by E. W. Carpenter of
Lancaster, Pa.

William J. Baader Collection

No. 1A16 Smooth Plane, Tabor Patent

1A16 SMOOTH PLANE, TABOR PATENT
This plane was made by the Tabor Plane Co. of New Bedford, Mass. and is
marked Pat'd Feb. 28, 85. The iron is held with a screw-type lever cap that is
quite short in comparison with the holding mechanism of most planes.

Jack Planes

The Jack-of-all-Trades and universal member of any tool chest is the jack
plane. They are from 15 to 18 inches long and the iron width is 1¾ to 2½
inches. Wider irons were available by special order at extra cost. These
planes were used for rapid removal of excess stock and for general rough
work. The iron of a true jack plane is ground to make a cut with a slight
hollow in the center. Rapid cutting with this type of iron is easier because the
chip can be thick in the center without tearing at the edges. Rough cuts with
the jack plane are followed by finish cuts with the other bench planes where
precision work is required. The wavy finish on the back side of old panels
and drawers is the result of a jack plane being used without any finish cut.
Many jack planes are noted to be ground essentially straight across to allow
them to produce a credible finished surface. The start on wood bodied jack

planes is located on the upper surface of the body forward of the iron. An open tote aft of the iron is characteristic of jack planes, however an occasional one is seen with a saw-type closed tote.

Even the name of the Jack plane provides a clue to its intended usage. Jack is a term applied to many mechanical contrivances designed for rough and coarse work. *Every Man His Own Mechanic* (Ref. 27) traces this usage of the term to the fact that Jack or Jaques was the most common Christian name in France and became a contemptuous expression for a common man. The term Jack was later applied to common tasks and tools; note the similar usage in such names as jack screw, boot jack, jack knife, and jack plane.

Except where noted on the individual descriptions, jack planes were made from beechwood.

1914 (Ref. 5)

No. 1B1 Jack Plane

1B1   JACK PLANE
This is the standard pattern jack plane offered by practically every plane supplier.
Length: 15 to 18 inches. A common length was 16 inches.
Iron Width: 1¾ to 2½ inches. A common width was 2¼ inches.
Iron Type: Single or double
Wood: Beech, apple, boxwood or rosewood
The open style tote and start location as shown in the illustration are almost universal features of jack planes made in America.

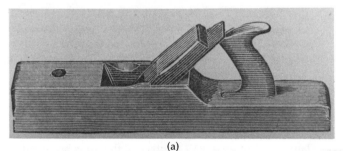

(a)

No. 1B2 Jack Plane, Razee

1914 (Ref. 5)

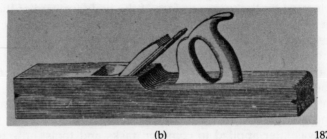

(b)   1877 (Ref. 29)
No. 1B2 Jack Plane, Razee

1B2   JACK PLANE, RAZEE
Also listed as a Recess Handle Plane and a Carpenter's Razee Jack Plane
Length: 16 inches
Iron Width: 2 to 2½ inches
Iron Type: Single or double
Most razee jack planes had the standard open style tote as shown in illustration (a). Illustration (b) shows a less common closed type tote.

The razee or cutaway jack plane is identical in function and in general size to the common pattern jack plane except for the lowered position of the tote. It would appear to the writer that lowering the tote allows a better balance and therefore more precise control of the tool. It is surprising that the razee did not become the more common of the two types.

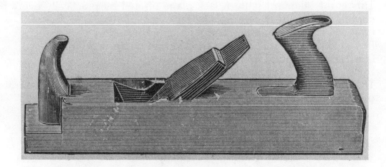

1914 (Ref. 5)
No. 1B3 Jack Plane, German Pattern

1B3   JACK PLANE, GERMAN PATTERN
Length: 16 inches approximately
Iron Type: Single or double
These planes were offered with a choice of the irons being either square or rounded on the upper end.

30

1914 (Ref. 5)

No. 1B4 Jack Plane, Double Razee

1B4 JACK PLANE, DOUBLE RAZEE
The term Double Razee is used for descriptive purposes only and was not used by the makers.

These planes were listed by Ohio Tool Company in 1901 as "Improved Wood Planes."
Length: 16 inches
Iron Width: 2⅛ inches
Iron Type: Double
Ohio Tool Company is the only manufacturer known to have made this type of plane.

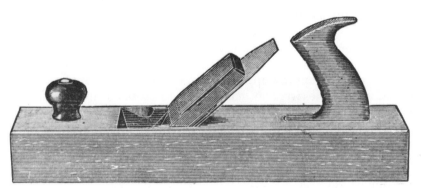

1914 (Ref. 5)

No. 1B5 Jack Plane, Front Knob

1B5 JACK PLANE, FRONT KNOB
Length: 15 or 16 inches
Iron Width: 2⅛ or 2¼ inches
Iron Type: Double
The front knob was coated with a heavy layer of black paint and was advertised as being "Ebonized."

No. 1B6 Jack Plane, Ship

1B6   JACK PLANE, SHIP
Length: 16 inches
Iron Width: 1¾ to 2⅛ inches
Iron Type: Double
The plane shown in the illustration was made by Thomas L. Appleton of Chelsea. It is 16 inches long and has a 1⅞ inch iron. The closed type tote used on this plane is normal for a fore or jointer plane but quite rare on a jack plane.

Fore Planes

The fore plane is the little brother to the jointer and is said by some writers to be called the fore plane because it is used before the jointer. Fore planes are from 18 to 24 inches long and have iron widths up to 2⅝ inches. Wider irons were available by special order at extra cost. Their purpose is to clean up the rough work done with the jack plane where a finer cut is required. The iron is ground almost straight across such that it would provide an even surface on a flat workpiece and could be used for most types of edge joining. The start is located on the upper surface of the plane body as on the jack plane. Saw-type totes were normally used because of the need for a firm grip to handle the weight. Fore planes are not as common as jack planes and jointers because many workmen did not own a complete set of bench planes and the fore plane was the one most apt to be omitted. There were also many helpers and handymen who made do with only smooth and jack planes.

The Bowles price list (Ref. 7) and the Collins broadside (Ref. 39) lists 21 and 22 inch bench planes as jointers rather than as fore planes. These references do not include the fore plane by name. It is tempting to conclude that these early listings were printed prior to common usage of the fore plane terminology, however two cases do not warrant a conclusion. It is worthy of note that both References 16 and 17 offer proof that the term Fore Plane was used in the early eighteen-fifties.

Except where noted on the individual descriptions, fore planes were made of beechwood.

No. 1C1 Fore Plane

1914 (Ref. 5)

1C1 FORE PLANE

This is the most common type of fore plane. It is sometimes called a Short Jointer and is occasionally listed as a Trying Plane.

Length: 18 to 24 inches. A common length was 22 inches

Iron Width: 2¼ to 2¾ inches. A common size was 2½ inches.

Iron Type: Single or double

Wood: Beech, apple, boxwood or rosewood. The rosewood fore planes were available on special order only.

No. 1C2 Fore Plane, Razee

1914 (Ref. 5)

1C2 FORE PLANE, RAZEE

Also listed as a Short Jointer, Carpenter's Razee Fore Plane or a Recess Handle Fore Plane.

Length: 18 to 24 inches. A common size was 22 inches.

Iron Width: 2⅛ to 2⅝ inches. A common size was 2⅜ inches.

Iron Type: Single or double

No. 1C3 Fore Plane, Double Razee

1914 (Ref. 5)

1C3 FORE PLANE, DOUBLE RAZEE

The term Double Razee is used for descriptive purposes only and was not used by the makers.

Length: 22 inches

Iron Width: 2⅜ inches

Iron Type: Double

No. 1C4 Fore Plane, Front Knob

1C4   FORE PLANE, FRONT KNOB
Length: 20 or 22 inches
Iron Width: 2⅜ or 2½ inches
Iron Type: Double
The front knob of this type plane had a thick coat of black paint and was advertised as being "ebonized."

This variety of fore plane has a thinner body and is considerably lighter in weight than the common fore plane. Note also the jack handle in lieu of the more conventional saw-type closed handle.

No. 02 SHIP PLANES, PER SET OF FOUR.

Prime Timber, Polished Lignum Vitæ Start.

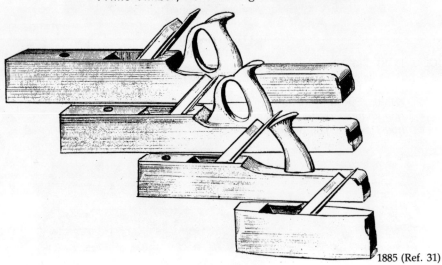

1885 (Ref. 31)

No. 1C5 Fore Plane, Ship

1C5   FORE PLANE, SHIP
Length: 22 inches
Iron Width: 2 to 2¼ inches
Iron Type: Double
The ship fore plane is the same as the razee fore plane except that the ship plane was normally sold with a narrower iron.

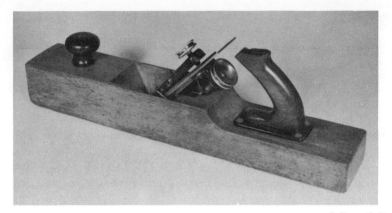

No. 1C6 Fore Plane, Rust Patent

1C6 FORE PLANE, RUST PATENT
Length: 18 inches
Iron Width: 2-5/16 inches
Patent number 287, 584 for the mechanism of this plane was granted to Solom R. Rust and Arthur E. Rust on Oct. 30, 1883. It is especially unique in that the cap iron, cutting iron and iron carriage are all fastened together and move as one unit when the iron is adjusted. The plane body is made of beechwood and provides an attractive contrast with the rosewood knob and tote. It is marked Standard Rule Co., Unionville, Conn. No. 28.

No. 1C7 Fore Plane, Double Wedge

1C7 FORE PLANE, DOUBLE WEDGE
This double wedge plane in marked "E.W. Carpenter Lancaster, Pa. PAT. Mar. 27, 1849." The bottom wedge is normally secured to the plane body with a screw but can be adjusted up and down to change the throat opening. Adjusting the two wedges will also result in a small variation of iron pitch.

Jointer Planes

The jointer, as its name implies, is the long plane that was used to make the final cut for fine quality edge joining. The longer length of the jointer allowed a straight edge-cut on a long workpiece without the tendency toward wavyness. Preparation of the workpiece was made by successive use of the jack and fore planes so that only one or two final passes were needed with the jointer. This limited use allowed the jointer to be kept exceptionally sharp and in top condition. Sizes are from 24 to 36 inches long with irons 2 to 3 inches wide. Ref. 7 listed 21 and 22 inch jointers, however fore planes were not included in that particular listing.

Planes of the jointer type that are in excess of 36 inches long are not uncommon. These longer planes were made commercially but were not listed or described in any available catalogs. Most suppliers listed jointer sizes in a choice of 26, 28 and 30 inches. Many of the jointer type planes longer than 30 inches were probably special ordered and intended for some specific use such as smoothing large floor areas, bridge timbers, etc. Planes of this type longer than 36 inches are arbitrarily listed as floor planes.

The iron of a jointer is ground perfectly straight across except for a slight break at the edges. Inasmuch as the edge of the iron need not engage the work, a perfect cut for edge joining could be obtained. Saw type totes are normally used on wood stock jointers as on the fore plane. The start is located in the upper edge of the body as in both the jack plane and fore plane.

Except where noted on the individual descriptions, jointer planes were made of beechwood.

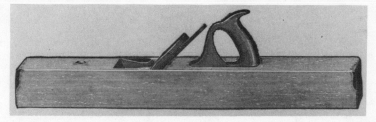

1914 (Ref. 5)

No. 1D1 Jointer Plane

1D1   JOINTER PLANE
    Also listed as a Long Jointer.
    Length: 24 to 36 inches. A common length was 26, 28 or 30 inches.
    Iron Width: 2¼ to 3 inches. A common size was 2⅝ inches.
    Iron Type: Single or double
    Wood: Beech, apple, boxwood or rosewood. The boxwood and rosewood planes were available on special order only.

1914 (Ref. 5)

No. 1D2 Jointer Plane, Razee

1D2   JOINTER PLANE, RAZEE
Also listed as a Razee Long Jointer, Recess Handle Jointer and a Carpenter's Razee Jointer.
Length: 24, 26, 28 or 30 inches
Iron Width   2¼ to 2¾ inches
Iron Type: Single or double

1914 (Ref. 5)

No. 1D3 Jointer Plane, Double Razee

1D3   JOINTER PLANE, DOUBLE RAZEE
The term Double Razee is used for descriptive purposes only and was not used by the suppliers.
Length: 26 or 28 inches
Iron Width: 2½ inches
Iron Type: Double

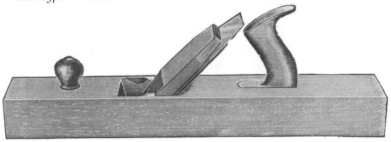

1914 (Ref. 5)

No. 1D4 Jointer Plane, Front Knob

1D4   JOINTER PLANE, FRONT KNOB
Length: 26, 28 and 30 inches
Iron Width: 2½ to 2⅝ inches
Iron Type: Double
The front knob was covered with a heavy coat of black paint and was advertised as being "Ebonized."

No. 1D5 Jointer Plane, Lightweight

1D5   JOINTER PLANE, LIGHTWEIGHT
This is a less expensive version of the common jointer.
Length: 26, 28 and 30 inches
Iron Width: 2½ inches
Iron Type: Double
The illustrated plane is 30 inches long and has a 2½ inch iron. Both plane and iron are marked Chipaway.

Thickness of the body on this plane is only 2¼ inches which accounts for a considerable reduction in weight when compared to the 3 inches or more thickness of the common jointer. Note also the open tote similar to those normally used on shorter tools such as jack planes.

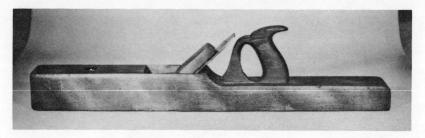

No. 1D6 Jointer Plane, Ship

1D6   JOINTER PLANE, SHIP
Length: 24 or 26 inches
Iron Width: 2 to 2½ inches
Iron Type: Double
Wood Type: Beech or lignum vitae
The plane shown in the illustration is a 26 inch Sandusky Tool Company jointer with a 2 inch iron.

General Purpose Planes

Numerical listing of general purpose planes.

Ref. No.	Name
2A1	Mitre Plane, Oval
2A2	Mitre Plane, Square
2A3	Mitre Plane, Worrall Patent
2A4	Mitre Plane, Picture Frame
2B1	Circular Plane
2B2	Circular Plane, Carriage Makers'
2C1	Toothing Plane
2C2	Toothing Plane, Handled
2D1	Scrub Plane, Horn
2E1	Chamfer Plane, Mander patent
2E2	Chamfer Plane
2E3	Chamfer Plane, Double
2F1	Beveling Plane
2G1	Ripping Plane
2H1	Badger
2J1	Floor Plane

Several varieties of planes are listed under the heading of General Purpose because they are used for multiple purposes or at least for more than one specific function.

Primary to this list are the mitre planes. They are much like the smooth planes in appearance except for the low blade angle. The iron is set low in these planes to allow trimming of end grain without chatter. Normal pitch for miter planes is about 35 degrees. They are generally seen with single irons although double iron types were stock-listed items. Most listings for mitre planes offered irons up to 1¾ inches wide with one listing of 2 inches. A second listing in some catalogs (References 11 and 14 for example) showed a "Block Mitre" plane with an iron width of 2 inches or more. These wider mitre planes may have been intended for use with a shoot board.

A second category of general purpose planes are the convex sole circular or compass planes. They are fairly well standardized as to size and appearance, however the sole curvature varies widely between makers. The variety of curvatures noted leads to the conclusion that there was not even a general attempt at standardization of this feature. The degree of curvature becomes even more baffling when it is realized that the supplier and makers catalogs did not specify the amount of curvature nor did they offer alternatives in this feature.

Toothing planes are included in the general purpose category because they were apparently used for different purposes by different owners. Adequate documentation exists to justify that these planes were used for smoothing knotty workpieces and also for roughing smooth surfaces prior to gluing, particularly in the application of veneer. These uses are discussed in detail in the June 1973 issue of *The Chronicle* (Ref. 24).

Sellens Collection

No. 2A1 Mitre Plane, Oval

2A1   MITRE PLANE, OVAL
Also listed as a Smooth Shape Mitre plane and occasionally as a Block plane
Length: Up to 12 inches
Iron Width: 1 to 2 inches
Iron Type: Single or double
Wood: Beech, boxwood, cocobola or rosewood
The plane shown in the illustration is stamped D.R. Barton & Co., Rochester, N.Y. It is 9½ inches long and has a 1¾ inch single iron. The iron is also marked D.R. Barton.

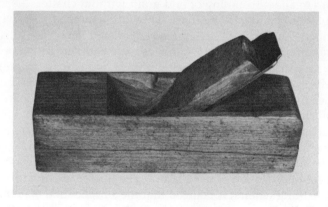

George Tuttle Collection

No. 2A2 Mitre Plane, Square

2A2 MITRE PLANE, SQUARE
Occasionally listed as a Block Plane.
Length: Up to 10 inches
Iron Width: 1½ to 2 inches
Iron Type: Single or double
Wood: Beech, boxwood, cocobola or rosewood.
The tool shown in the illustration is a 9 inch plane made by Greenfield Tool,
Greenfield, Mass. The 1¾ inch single iron is stamped Hancock Tool Co.

Roger K. Smith Collection

No. 2A3 Mitre Plane, Worrall Patent

2A3 MITRE PLANE, WORRALL PATENT
The iron of the illustrated plane is secured by tightening the bolt in the heel.
The plane was made by the Multiform Moulding Plane Company of Boston
and is marked as having been made under a patent granted Aug. 29, 1854.
The patent reference was probably an early patent of Thomas D. Worrall,
however the 1854 Worrall patent dealt with the idea of a detachable sole
rather than an iron retention device. Worrall did patent the thru-bolt idea of
iron retention under a later grant. These and other Worrall patents are
discussed by William B. Hilton in the July 1975 issue of *The Chronicle* (Ref. 24).

The illustrated plane is 9 inches long and has a 1¾ inch iron.

1889 (Ref. 33)

No. 2A4 Mitre Plane, Picture Frame

2A4   MITRE PLANE, PICTURE FRAME

Also listed as a Shooting Plane, Schuting Plane and as a Picture Frame Jointer.

Length: 24 to 36 inches

Iron Width: 3, 3½, 4 inches

This type of plane was intended to make precision cuts such as needed for a picture frame corner or similar joint. The workpiece was held rigidly against a stop and the plane was made to slide in a fixed groove. The shooting board or table could be purchased with the plane or constructed by the owner to match. The iron was usually set extra fine in a narrow throat.

The illustrated plane is a double picture frame jointer complete with matching table. The table is 36 inches long.

Sellens Collection

No. 2B1 Circular Plane

2B1   CIRCULAR PLANE

Also listed as Smooth Plane-Circular, Compass Plane, Compass Plane-Smooth and as a Heel Plane.

The circular plane was used wherever curved members were required. Furniture making was the primary usage.

Length: The length was not specified in any available catalog.
     Noted lengths are 7 to 9 inches.

Iron Width: 2 to 2⅝ inches. A common size was 2½ inches.

Iron Type: Single or double

Wood: Beech

The plane shown in the illustration is stamped P. Brooks & Co., Pittsfield. It is 7¾ inches long and has a 2 inch Barry and Way single iron.

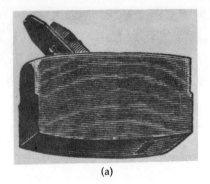

(a)   1880 (Ref. 15)

(b)   Sellens Collection
No. 2B2 Circular Plane, Carriage Makers'

2B2   CIRCULAR PLANE, CARRIAGE MAKERS'
Listed by one supplier as Carriage Makers' Smooth, Circle Face.
Length: Length was not specified in the catalogs.
        Planes noted are 7 inches or shorter.
Iron Width: 1½ or 1⅝ inches
Iron Type: Double
Wood: Beech
The plane shown in illustration (b) was made by H. Wells, Wms. Burg, Mass.
It is 6⅜ inches long and has a 1½ inch Moulson Brothers double iron.

No. 2C1 Toothing Plane

2C1   TOOTHING PLANE
Also listed as a Tooth Plane and as a Veneer Smoothing Plane.
Length: Not specified in the catalogs. Planes noted are generally 7 to 9 inches
      in length.
Iron Width: 1⅝ to 2⅝ inches. A common width was 2 inches.
Wood: Beech or apple
The iron of a toothing plane is always set high. Pitch is a minimum of 60
degrees and is sometimes a full 90 degrees.

This type of plane was offered with a brass sole at extra cost.

The toothing plane shown in the illustration is a No. 30 made by Ohio Tool
Company. It is 7 inches long. The iron is also marked Ohio Tool Company
and has 26 teeth per inch.

No. 2C2 Toothing Plane, Handled

2C2   TOOTHING PLANE, HANDLED
The illustrated plane was made by John Veit of Philadelphia. This type has
not been noted in any catalog or broadside.

44

No. 2D1 Scrub Plane, Horn

2D1 SCRUB PLANE, HORN
Also listed as a Horn Smooth Scrub Plane
Length: Approximately 8 inches
Iron Width: 1¼ to 2 inches
Iron Type: Single
The iron of a scrub plane is ground to a convex shape for rapid removal of excess material from the workpiece. It was followed by a smooth plane if an even surface was desired.

The illustrated plane is 8¼ inches long and has a 1¼ inch single iron. It was made by Chapin-Stevens Union Factory. The neat patch on the horn is an example of the excellent craftmanship of the present owner.

George Tuttle Collection

No. 2E1 Chamfer Plane, Mander Patent

2E1   CHAMFER PLANE, MANDER PATENT

The illustrated chamfer plane is marked Mander & Dillin Manf'd Phila, Pat'd Mar 24, 85. Patent number 314,338 was granted to James Mander for the unique method of iron adjustment. Depth of the chamfer is regulated by adjustment of the second wedge which is held in place by a screw on each side of the plane. Planes from 6 to 7 inches long have been noted. Overall width of the plane body is approximately 2¾ inches.

W.L. Gordon Collection

No. 2E2 Chamfer Plane

2E2   CHAMFER PLANE

Length: 6½ inches
Iron Width: 1¼ inches

This type of chamfer plane can be adjusted by positioning a movable fence on the sole. The illustrated plane was made in London by Melhuish on Fetter Lane.

Sellens Collection

No. 2E3 Chamfer Plane, Double

2E3   CHAMFER PLANE, DOUBLE
This type of plane was listed by Mathieson & Sons of Glasgow as a Champhering or V Plane.
The illustrated tool was made by Hields, Nottingham. American maker lists do not include this type of plane.

George Tuttle Collection

No. 2F1 Beveling Plane

2F1   BEVELING PLANE
This unique patented plane will cut a bevel on both corners of a workpiece with one pass. The two 1¼ inch irons are adjustable sideways to obtain any oblique angle greater than 90 degrees and a screw stop is incorporated to control the depth of cut. Length of the sole is 10½ inches. The plane is marked M. B. Tidey & Co., Dundee, N.Y. patd July 4, 1854. Patent number 11,235 was assigned to this tool.

1885 (Ref. 31)

No. 2G1 Ripping Plane

2G1   RIPPING PLANE
Listed as Kinney's Patent Gauge Ripping Plane.
Wood: Beech or apple.
The cutting is done by an adjustable rotating wheel. The wheel can be seen
below the plane body in the illustration.

Sellens Collection

No. 2H1 Badger

2H1   BADGER
Also listed as a Carpenters' Badger.
Length: 16 inches approximately
A badger is essentially the same as a jack plane except that the iron is skewed
and canted such that it runs out at the lower right corner of the plane body. It
was used for cutting the tapered edge of a panel and could be used to cut a

wide rabbet or for general purpose bench work. The skew iron was less likely to tear the wood when cutting cross grain at the end of the panel particularly at the start and finish of the cut. This type plane was never popular in America and many makers did not even list them. Panel work was done primarily with the wide variety of tools called raising planes. The badger was occasionally provided with a side spur and a bottom fence but usually had neither of these refinements.

The illustrated plane was made by E. Smith of Worcester. A previous owner had added a brass side stop of the kind normally used on a common filletster. The stop was notched into the plane as can be seen in the photo.

No. 2J1 Floor Plane

2J1   FLOOR PLANE
Planes of the bench jointer type longer than 36 inches are called Floor Planes here-in. The definition is somewhat arbitrary inasmuch as some writers and collectors refer to any bench type jointer longer than 30 inches as a floor plane. It is true that most suppliers offered standard jointers up to 30 inches only but there was an occasional listing of 32, 34 and 36 inches. The term "Floor Plane" has not been noted in any catalog or makers' literature. It is possible that these planes were all special order items.
Length: Longer than 36 inches
Iron Type: Single or double
The illustrated plane is 40 inches long and has a 2⅞ inch iron. It was made by Sandusky Tool Company. This plane and two others of the same length were among the tools of a small contractor who specialized in laying high quality floors such as gymnasiums and bowling alleys. It is possible that this is the plane listed as a Tank Jointer by two of the larger plane making firms. The term probably referred to a large jointer used in making the huge wooden tanks commonly seen in older oil fields.

49

Special Purpose Planes

Numerical listing of special purpose planes.

Ref. No.	NAME
3A1	Sash Plane, One Iron
3A2	Sash Plane, Two Irons
3A3	Sash Plane, Two Irons, Handled
3A4	Sash Plane, Screw Arm
3A5	Sash Plane, Screw Arm, Handled
3A6	Sash Plane, Thumb Screw
3A7	Sash Plane, Diamond Pad
3A8	Sash Plane, Wedge Arm
3A9	Sash Plane, Handled
3B1	Nosing Plane, One Iron
3B2	Nosing Plane, One Iron, Solid Handle
3B3	Nosing Plane, One Iron, Applied Handle
3B4	Nosing Plane, Two Irons
3B5	Nosing Plane, Two Irons, Handled
3B6	Nosing Plane, Center Throat
3C1	Table Planes
3C2	Table Planes with Fence
3D1	Raising Plane
3D2	Raising Plane, Side Stop
3D3	Raising Plane, Full Length Stop
3D4	Raising Jack Plane
3D5	Raising Plane, Screw Arm
3E1	Pump Plane
3E2	Pump Plane, Handled
3F1	Gutter Plane
3G1	Coping Plane
3G2	Coping Plane, Double
3H1	Spar Plane
3J1	Oar Plane
3J2	Oar Plane, Jack Shape
3J3	Oar Plane, Skew
3K1	Washboard Plane
3L1	Hand Rail Planes
3L2	Hand Rail Planes
3L3	Hand Rail Plane, Handled
3M1	Toy Planes
3M2	Toy Planes
3N1	Cigar Lighter Plane
3P1	Router, Old Woman's Tooth
3P2	Router, Old Woman's Tooth
3P3	Carriage Makers' Router
3P4	Carriage Makers' Router, Double
3R1	Door Plane, Single

3R2	Door Plane, Double
3R3	Door Plane, Double
3R4	Door Plane, Screw Arm
3S1	Whip Plane
3T1	Meeting Rail Plane
3U1	Basket Shave
3V1	Carriage Makers' Jarvis
3W1	Weatherstrip Planes, Pair

The wide category of planes listed under the Special Purpose heading is actually comprised of the miscellaneous items that do not fit within the other general headings. These planes were generally sold for a specific purpose and are not well suited for any general application.

All of the special purpose planes were listed as being made of beechwood except as noted on the individual description pages.

Sash Planes

The sash plane is a specialized tool used in making windows. It is actually a combination of a rabbet and a moulding plane fashioned such that both cuts are made at the same time. One side cuts the rabbet for the glass and the other side cuts the decorative inside moulding. The various moulding patterns that were available are shown in the Sash Plane Pattern sketches. The Ovolo and Bevel patterns were most often listed as available in stock.

The adjustable sashes were available with and without self regulating features. In the case of a screw-arm sash or equivalent, self regulating meant that one half of the plane body was threaded and the head of the screw was captive in the other half of the plane body. Rotating the screw arms would force the two halves of the plane apart and hold them in position. The purpose of the screw arm nut was merely to lock the screw against further rotation. Those planes without the self regulating feature had to be shimmed apart to keep the two halves properly spaced.

Sash planes with handles were catalogued by several makers but are relatively scarce.

The standard sash was made to work 1 1/2 inch stock but sizes could be ordered to work thicknesses from 1 3/16 to 2 inches.

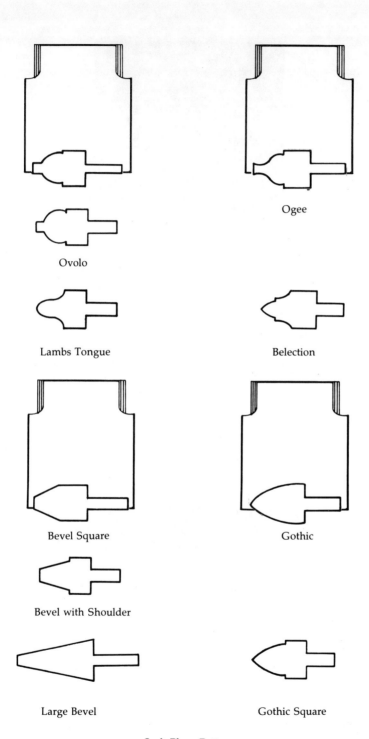

Ovolo

Ogee

Lambs Tongue

Belection

Bevel Square

Gothic

Bevel with Shoulder

Large Bevel

Gothic Square

Sash Plane Patterns

53

No. 3A1 Sash Plane, One Iron

3A1   SASH PLANE, ONE IRON
      Length: 9½ inches approximately
      Patterns: Bevel, ovolo, gothic or ogee.
      Available full boxed, single boxed or without box strips

The tool shown in the illustration is an ovolo pattern sash marked G. F. Seybold CINTO. It is 9½ inches long and is made to work 1½ inch stock. The 8/8 marked on the heel apparently refers to the thickness of stock not including the depth of the rabbet.

1872 (Ref. 18)

No. 3A2 Sash Plane, Two Irons

3A2   SASH PLANE, TWO IRONS
      Length: 9½ inches approximately
      Patterns: Bevel, ovolo, gothic, ogee or nosing. The nosing pattern was also
         called Showcase.
      Available full boxed, single boxed or without box strips. This type of sash was
      also available with brass plating.

54

No. 3A3 Sash Plane, Two Irons, Handled

3A3   SASH PLANE, TWO IRONS, HANDLED
Length: 11½ inches
Wood Type: Beech or boxwood
The illustrated plane is a bevel pattern. Handled sash planes were listed by several suppliers but are seldom seen in collections.

(a)   Sellens Collection

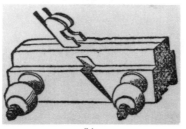

(b)   1897 (Ref. 10)
No. 3A4 Sash Plane, Screw Arm

3A4   SASH PLANE, SCREW ARM
Also called a Moving Sash with Screw Arms. This is the most common type of
sash plane.
Length: 9½ inches approximately
Wood Type: Beech, boxwood or rosewood
Patterns: Bevel, ovolo, gothic or ogee
Available full boxed, single boxed or without box strips. These planes were
also available with brass plating and could be bought with and without the
self-regulating feature.

The screw-arm sash shown in illustration (a) was made by Ohio Tool Co. It is
the standard 9½ inches long and is made to work 1½ inch or thicker stock.
This plane is marked No. 128 on the heel and is self-regulating.

Donald Wing Collection

No. 3A5 Sash Plane, Screw Arm, Handled

3A5   SASH PLANE, SCREW ARM, HANDLED
Length: 11½ inches approximately
The illustrated plane is made of boxwood.

Sellens Collection

No. 3A6 Sash Plane, Thumb Screw

3A6 **SASH PLANE, THUMB SCREW**
Sometimes listed as a Brass Screw Sash.
Length: 9½ inches approximately
Wood Type: Beech
Patterns: Bevel, ovolo, gothic or ogee.
Available full boxed or single boxed. This type of sash is self regulating.

The illustrated brass-screw sash is a bevel pattern and is marked A. B. Semple & Bro., Louisville, K. Y. It is the standard 9½ inches long.

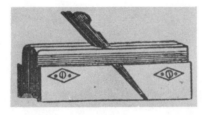

1872 (Ref. 18)

No. 3A7 Sash Plane, Diamond Pad

3A7 **SASH PLANE, DIAMOND PAD**
Also listed as a Moving Sash-Diamond Pad.
Length: 9½ inches approximately
Patterns: Ovolo, gothic, ogee, or bevel.
The diamond pad inserts were made of brass with steel adjusting screws.
Available with single, double or full box strips.

George Tuttle Collection

No. 3A8 Sash Plane, Wedge Arm

3A8   SASH PLANE, WEDGE ARM
Adjustable sash planes with the wedge type locking are relatively scarce
when compared to the screw arm type. Available catalogs did not list this
type by name, however at least two of the earlier lists contained a Moving
Sash in addition to the Screw Arm variety. It is reasonable to assume that
these listings refered to wedge arm type planes. In any case, the wedge type
sashes can be assumed to be among the older American-made planes.

The sash plane shown in the illustration is stamped Chapin and Kendall,
Baltimore. It is a bevel pattern without box strips and is 9½ inches long.

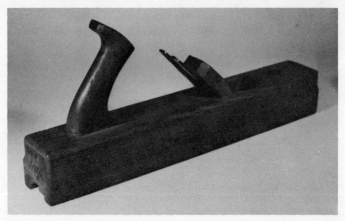

George Tuttle Collection

No. 3A9 Sash Plane, Handled

3A9   SASH PLANE, HANDLED
A unique variety of handled sash is shown in the illustration. This plane has
two irons held by a single wedge. The plane body is 14⅜ inches long. The
mark on the toe is S. Noyes.

Nosing Planes

Rounding the front edge of a stair tread calls for the use of a nosing plane. Standard sizes of nosings were made in 10 widths to work stock from ¾ inch to 2 inches thick. In addition, 4 listings down to ¼ inch have been noted in the trade catalogs, however the exact usage of the smaller sizes has not been determined. The numerical size stamped on the heel refers to the diameter of the cut.

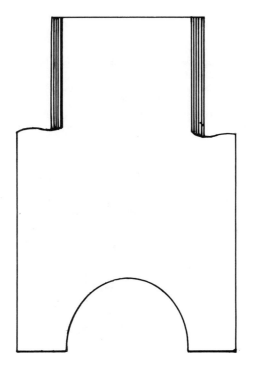

Nosing Plane Contour

1857 (Ref. 13)

No. 3B1 Nosing Plane, One Iron

3B1 NOSING PLANE, ONE IRON
Also listed as a Step Plane, Stair Plane and as a Nosing Step Plane
Length: 9½ inches approximately
Width of Cut: ¼, ⅜, ½, ⅝, ¾, ⅞, 1, 1⅛, 1¼, 1⅜, 1½, 1⅝, 1¾, 2 inches.
 Common sizes are 1 and 1¼ inches.
The single iron nosing plane shown in the illustration is an Ohio Tool
Company No. 90. It is the standard 9½ inches long and makes a 1½ inch
diameter cut.

No. 3B2 Nosing Plane, One Iron, Solid Handle

3B2 NOSING PLANE, ONE IRON, SOLID HANDLE
Also listed as a Step Plane, Stair Plane or as a Nosing Step Plane.
Length: 12 inches approximately
Width of Cut: ¾, ⅞, 1, 1⅛, 1¼, 1⅜, 1½, 1⅝, 1¾, 2 inches. Common sizes
 are 1 and 1¼ inches
The nosing plane shown in the illustration is marked Hills & Winship,
Springfield, Ms. It is 11½ inches long and makes a 1¼ inch diameter cut.

No. 3B3 Nosing Plane, One Iron, Applied Handle

3B3   NOSING PLANE, ONE IRON, APPLIED HANDLE
        Also listed as a Step Plane, Stair Plane or as a Nosing Step Plane
        Length: 12 inches approximately
        Width of Cut: ¾, ⅞, 1, 1⅛, 1¼, 1⅜, 1½, 1⅝, 1¾, 2 inches
        The illustrated plane is an Ohio Tool Company No. 90½. It is 12 inches long
        and makes a 1 inch diameter cut.

No. 3B4 Nosing Plane, Two Irons

3B4   NOSING PLANE, TWO IRONS
        Also listed as a Step Plane, Stair Plane or as a Nosing Step Plane. This is the
        most common type of nosing plane.
        Length: 9½ inches approximately
        Width of Cut: ½, ¾, ⅞, 1, 1⅛, 1¼, 1⅜, 1½, 1⅝, 1¾, 2 inches. Common
            sizes are 1 and 1¼ inches.
        The two iron nosing plane shown in the illustration is an Ohio Tool Company
        No. 91. It is 9½ inches long and makes a 1¼ inch diameter cut.

61

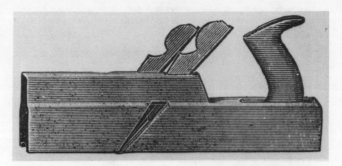

1914 (Ref. 5)

No. 3B5 Nosing Plane, Two Irons, Handled

3B5   NOSING PLANE, TWO IRONS, HANDLED
       Also listed as a Step Plane, Stair Plane or as a Nosing Step Plane
       Length: 12 inches approximately
       Width of Cut: ¾, ⅞, 1, 1¼, 1⅜, 1½, 1⅝, 1¾, 2 inches

Sellens Collection

No. 3B6 Nosing Plane, Center Throat

3B6   NOSING PLANE, CENTER THROAT
       Length: 14½ inches
       Size: 1⅛ inches
       This is a scarce pattern of the nosing plane. Most nosings have the simple side
       opening for the discharge of shavings.

Table Planes

These planes were made specifically to cut the matching edges between the leaf and the top of a drop-leaf table. Several catalogs listed a gauge for fifteen cents extra that was made to check the work of a particular set of table planes. The gauge was furnished with the planes in some cases.

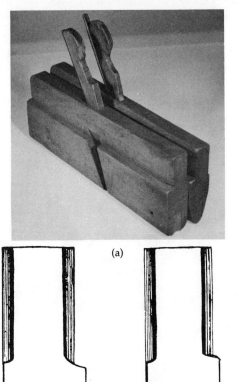

(a)

Sellens Collection

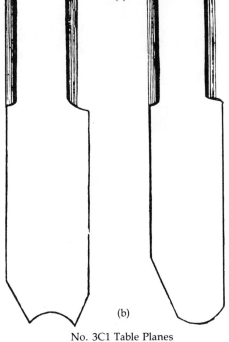

(b)

1857 (Ref. 13)

No. 3C1 Table Planes

3C1 TABLE PLANES
Also called Table Hollows and Rounds
Length: 9½ inches approximately
Size of Iron: ⅜, ½, ⅝, ¾, ⅞ inches. Size stamped on the heel refers to the diameter of the cut.

These planes were always sold in pairs and were available full boxed and plain.

The table planes shown in illustration (a) were made by Hall, Case & Co., Columbus, Ohio. They are full boxed as can be seen in the photo and are the standard 9½ inches long. Diameter of the cut measures exactly ½ inch which agrees with the 4/8 marked on the heel of both planes. The irons on this pair are set at a relatively high 60 degrees. It has been noted that most table planes have the irons set at 55 to 60 degrees instead of the 45 degree pitch of the common moulding planes.

The cutting surfaces of table planes span a greater portion of the arc than standard hollow and round planes of the same size. Note also that the hollow shown in illustration (b) is tapered on both sides near the cutting surface rather than on one side only as in a common hollow. Common hollows and rounds are generally not boxed.

(a)   George Tuttle Collection

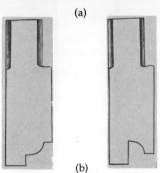

(b)   1857 (Ref. 13)

No. 3C2 Table Planes with Fence

64

3C2 TABLE PLANES WITH FENCE

Also called Table Hollows and Rounds with Fence

Length: 9½ inches approximately

Size of Iron: ½, ⅝, ¾, ⅞ inches. Size stamped on the heel refers to the diameter of the cut.

These planes were available full boxed or plain and were always sold in pairs.

The pair of table planes shown in illustration (a) were made by Bensen & Crannell of Albany. Diameter of the curve is slightly less than ½ inch.

Raising Planes

The function of a raising plane is to thin the edge of a panel thus making the center of the panel stand out. This was called raising a panel. The several varieties of raising planes have the common features of a wide flat sole with the iron set at a skew. The skewed iron was necessary for making the cross grain cuts at the ends of the panel. A straight set iron would have a tendency to tear the wood rather than make a clean cut. The wide iron was characteristic of a raising plane simply because a narrow raising plane would be essentially the same as a common filletster. Many advanced tool collectors erroneously refer to a raising plane as a large filletster.

Differences between makers regarding terminology used to identify raising and panel planes make firm identification difficult. The raising planes have been positively identified in more than one catalog by comparison of makers numbers with actual planes. The problem arises because some suppliers referred to "raising or panel planes" while other suppliers listed raising and panel separately at slightly different prices. Panel planes were generally the least expensive of the two and were therefore probably narrower and/or shorter than the standard raising plane.

Sellens Collection

No. 3D1 Raising Plane

3D1   RAISING PLANE
      Also listed as a Panel Plane.
      This is one of the simpler varieties of a raising plane inasmuch as a side stop is
      not provided.
      Length: 14 to 16 inches
      Size: Seven sizes were available as follows: 2¼, 2½, 2¾, 3, 3¼, 3½, 4 inches
      These planes were available with and without a spur cutter.

      The illustrated plane has a 3½ inch iron and was made by Child, Pratt & Co.
      of St. Louis, Mo.

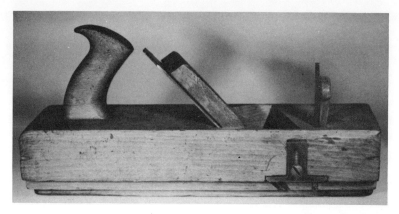

No. 3D2 Raising Plane, Side Stop

3D2   RAISING PLANE, SIDE STOP
Length: 14 to 16 inches
Size: Seven sizes were available as follows: 2¼, 2½, 2¾, 3, 3¼, 3½, 4 inches
These planes were available with and without a spur cutter and were also available boxed.

The illustrated plane is a No. 114 made by Ohio Tool Co.

No. 3D3 Raising Plane, Full Length Stop

3D3   RAISING PLANE, FULL LENGTH STOP
Also listed as a Panel Plane.
Length: 14 to 16 inches
Size: Seven sizes were available as follows: 2¼, 2½, 2¾, 3, 3¼, 3½, 4 inches
The illustrated plane is marked R. L. Jones, Williamsburgh, Mass. It has a 3 inch iron.

1872 (Ref. 18)

No. 3D4 Raising Jack Plane

3D4   RAISING JACK PLANE

Also listed as a Panel or Pannel Plane.

Width: Width was not specified in any of the available catalogs. Items noted have iron widths of approximately 2 inches. Both width and length are about the same as a common jack plane which probably accounts for the name.

Length: Approximately 16 inches.

This type of plane was available with and without a spur cutter and a moving fence.

George Tuttle Collection

No. 3D5 Raising Plane, Screw Arms

3D5   RAISING PLANE, SCREW ARMS

Also listed as a Panel Plane.

Size: Seven sizes were available as follows: 2¼, 2½, 2¾, 3, 3¼, 3½, 4 inches The illustrated plane is a No. 115 made by Ohio Tool Co. It is 15 inches long and has a 2½ inch iron.

Marion Henley Collection

No. 3D6 Panel Plane

3D6   PANEL PLANE
This type of plane has a narrow slanted sole and a fixed fence. These features are characteristic of many homemade panel planes but have not been noted in any commercial literature.

William J. Baader Collection

No. 3E1 Pump Plane

3E1   PUMP PLANE
Length: 9½ inches
Width of Cut: Will cut a half-circular groove 1¼ inches in diameter.
The illustrated plane is a No. 32½ made by Ohio Tool Co. It is listed in the 1901 catalog (Ref. 1) as a pump plane and is cross-referenced in the 1885 Sandusky catalog (Ref. 31) as a pump plane for chain pumps. This type of plane was available for a long period of time but is one of the scarcer varieties of wooden planes.

69

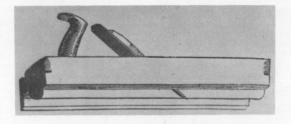

1872 (Ref. 18)

No. 3E2 Pump Plane, Handled

3E2   PUMP PLANE, HANDLED
This plane was listed by one supplier as being suitable for chain pumps.
Width of Cut: 1 to 1½ inches. Cuts a half circle groove.
The 1872 Greenfield Tool Company Catalog (Ref. 18) has the captions re-
versed between the pump and gutter planes thus indicating that this tool is
called a gutter plane.

1872 (Ref. 18)

No. 3F1 Gutter Plane

3F1   GUTTER PLANE
The gutter plane, as its name implies, is a rounded bottom plane used for
hollowing out gutters, troughs and similar long curved sections. It is essentially a jack plane with a curved bottom. In fact, most of the gutter planes
noted in collections are modified jack planes or are completely homemade.
Many of these tools can be identified as reworked jack planes by reference to
the manufacturers series number on the heel of the plane. It is speculated that
worn or damaged jack planes may have been converted to gutter planes
rather than being discarded.
Length: 15 to 16 inches
Width of Iron: 1½ to 2⅝ inches

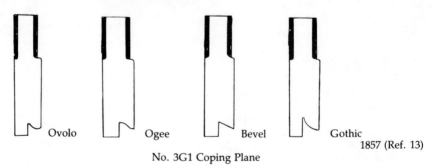

Ovolo   Ogee   Bevel   Gothic

1857 (Ref. 13)

No. 3G1 Coping Plane

3G1 COPING PLANE

Also called Sash Coping Plane or Single Coping Plane
Length: 9½ inches approximately
Available boxed or plain

Coping planes were used to undercut the bottom and top rails of a window sash such that they would join snugly with the moulded side stiles. They could also be used to make a similar cut on the dividing rails between window panes. These planes were sold to match each pattern of sash plane inasmuch as the coping cut must be the reverse of the moulding cut made by the sash plane. Four patterns are illustrated above.

(a)   George Tuttle Collection

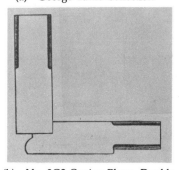

1857 (Ref. 13)

(b)   No. 3G2 Coping Plane, Double

3G2 COPING PLANE, DOUBLE

Also called Sash Coping Plane, Double
Length: 9½ inches approximately
These planes were available in an ovolo, ogee, gothic or bevel pattern. They were listed either plain or boxed.

The double coping plane shown in illustration (a) is a bevel pattern and is 9½ inches long. It is marked S. Brown on the toe.

No. 3H1 Spar Plane

3H1   SPAR PLANE
Length: 7 inches approximately
Width of Iron: 2¼ inches approximately
Type of Iron: Single or double
A spar plane has a very slight side-to-side curvature to allow it to work timbers several inches in diameter. Several planes noted in collections are curved to fit the arc of a circle 6 to 8 inches across.

No. 3J1 Oar Plane

3J1   OAR PLANE
Length: 7 inches approximately
Width of Iron: 2 inches approximately
Type of Iron: Single or double
The oar plane is curved to cut a small diameter circle as would be required to fashion an oar. The degree of curvature is the primary difference between oar and spar planes.

72

1885 (Ref. 31)

No. 3J2 Oar Plane, Jack Shape

3J2   OAR PLANE, JACK SHAPE
Sandusky Tool Co. (Ref. 31) provided the only available illustration of this type plane. It would appear from the illustration that the iron curvature spans roughly 60 degrees of arc which is the same as that of a standard pattern hollow. This amount of curve would allow working timbers up to 4 inches in diameter if we assume that the iron is approximately two inches wide.

Donald Wing Collection

No. 3J3 Oar Plane, Skew

3J3   OAR PLANE, SKEW
This unique oar plane with a skew iron is approximately 16 inches long and has a 2¾ inch iron.

(a)   George Tuttle Collection

(b)   William J. Baader Collection

No. 3K1 Washboard Plane

3K1   WASHBOARD PLANE
Washboard planes were listed by several suppliers, however none of the
noted catalogs included an illustration or even a word of description. Commercially made planes of this type are quite scarce even in the larger collections. The paucity of information prevents an accurate general description.

Illustration (a) shows a 9 inch washboard plane marked W. Steele, Wheeling.
It has a 1⅛ inch iron.

The two planes shown in illustration (b) are the standard 9½ inches long and
are essentially identical. One was made by Hall-Case and the other was made
by Ohio Tool Co.

No. 3L1 Hand Rail Planes

3L1   HAND RAIL PLANES
Several American makers listed hand rail planes separately and in pairs. However, none of the available catalogs offer either a description or an illustration of these tools. They were offered with either single or double irons and either with or without handles. Three patterns were available to cut ogee, round or ovolo shaped rails.

The excellent pair shown in the illustration are good examples of hand rail planes. They are 6⅝ inches long and have 1¾ inch irons. The fences on the bottom are adjustable to allow working various size rails. Double irons are provided as can be seen in the illustration. The cap irons are ground to the same contour as the cutting irons. These planes were made in England and are included due to a lack of American made examples of adjustable type hand rail planes.

No. 3L2 Hand Rail Planes

75

3L2　HAND RAIL PLANES

A pair of non-adjustable hand rail planes are shown in the illustration. They are notched at the heel such that the sole is essentially shortened. This design allowed for a short sole as needed to work around curves without reducing the length needed for a firm two-handed grasp of the tool.

Sellens Collection

No. 3L3 Hand Rail Plane, Handled

3L3　HAND RAIL PLANE, HANDLED

This type of plane was neither illustrated nor adequately described in American catalogs. The illustrated example is 13 inches long and has a 2¼ inch single iron. The slotted fence is adjustable over a short span by loosening two screws. The screws can also be moved to different holes in the sole thereby allowing further adjustment of the fence.

Marion Henley Collection

No. 3M1 Toy Planes

3M1　TOY PLANES

These small planes were made in various sizes for inclusion in toy tool boxes. The tool boxes were offered in different sizes hence the different sizes of planes. The larger one in the illustration is 7 inches long and has a 1⅛ inch iron. The short plane is 5½ inches long and has a 1 inch iron. The start pin on these planes is located ahead of the iron as shown in the illustration. The pin is actually a short tack with an iron head. The single irons were relatively soft and were obviously made to be toys only. The wooden parts were beech and were well made except that the corner chamfers and reliefs were small or omitted entirely. These planes did not have a makers mark.

Jack   1914 (Ref. 5)   Smooth   1914 (Ref. 5)

Trying   1889 (Ref. 32)

No. 3M2 Toy Planes   Sellens Collection

3M2 TOY PLANES
Width of Iron: 1¼ to 1¾ inches
Length: Smooth plane 4 to 6 inches
          Jack plane 7 to 12 inches
          Trying plane 9 to 12 inches
Several plane catalogs listed toy smooth and jack planes. V. A. Emond & Co. (Ref. 32) was the only firm which listed a toy trying plane, however one other plane list included fore and jointer planes under the heading of toys. These planes were sold primarily for inclusion in the higher priced toy tool boxes. Other than size, the soft iron in place of the tempered cutting iron was the major difference between these and actual working tools. Note also the lack of chamfers on the toy smooth plane illustrated.

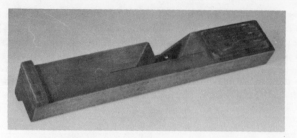

No. 3N1 Cigar Lighter Plane

3N1   CIGAR LIGHTER PLANE
Length: 9¼ inches
The illustrated plane was designed to make curled shavings that could be used to transfer a flame from the fireplace to your cigar or pipe. The name and instruction placard are still pasted to the plane. Planes for this purpose are generally called Spill Planes and are usually homemade in a wide variety of sizes and shapes. They were listed commercially in Europe but have not been noted on any American plane sales literature.

No. 3P1 Router, Old Woman's Tooth

3P1   ROUTER, OLD WOMAN'S TOOTH
Most of the Old Woman's Tooth Routers seen in America are homemade and are quite often made from a section of moulded stair rail. They are generally five to eight inches wide. This type of tool was offered commercially in Europe but has not been noted in lists published by the American makers.

The illustrated tool is of English manufacture and is 5½ inches wide. The iron is 9/16 inches wide and appears to be a standard plow iron.

78

1905 (Ref. 35)

No. 3P2 Router, Old Woman's Tooth

3P2 ROUTER, OLD WOMAN'S TOOTH
This type of router is seen quite often in the United States but most, if not all, are of English origin. The illustration is taken from *The Handyman's Book* (Ref. 35) which states "The router, or old woman's tooth, is a kind of plane used for working out the bottom of rectangular cavities; it is used for cutting cross grooves in timber to a certain depth, particularly when the groove does not go the whole width of the stuff, as for instance, with sinkings in treads and risers in strings. It has a broad sole, and its cutter projects the depth of the required sinking."

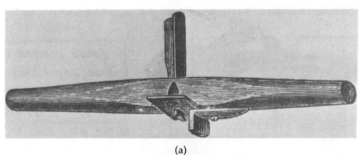

(a)

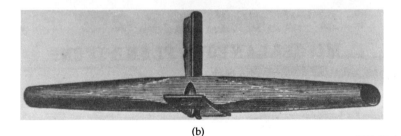

(b)

1880 (Ref. 15)

No. 3P3 Carriage Makers' Router

3P3 CARRIAGE MAKERS' ROUTER
This type of router has a straight stock with a narrow cutting iron in the center. The center section of the sole is normally plated to reduce wear. The tool was used to clean out a rabbet in a curved section or to make a curved

79

groove for inlay or other decoration. The iron is often made in the form of a C curve or hook.

The tool shown in illustration (a) has a double edged iron that will cut in either direction and an adjustable fence or guard. A single edged variety was made with a fence that could be easily removed and attached on the opposite side of the iron. Illustration (b) shows a similar tool offered without a fence.

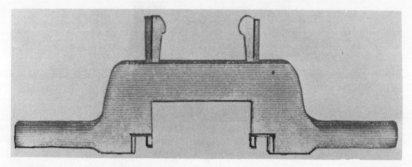

1877 (Ref. 9)

No. 3P4 Carriage Makers' Router, Double

3P4   CARRIAGE MAKERS' ROUTER, DOUBLE
The double router has two symmetrical irons designed to let the tool be used on either the right or left hand side of the workpiece. Its purpose is the same as that of the single router. This type of tool is relatively scarce and most examples noted in collections are homemade.

Herman Maddocks Collection

No. 3R1 Door Plane, Single

3R1   DOOR PLANE, SINGLE
This plane is constructed to cut the groove and the moulding on one side for letting in a door panel or similar insert. The illustrated plane cuts a 3/16 groove. Separate irons are used to plow the groove and to cut the moulding. Planes of this type were listed in sizes of ½ to ⅝ inches which probably referred to the width of the moulding cut.

No. 3R2 Door Plane, Double

3R2   DOOR PLANE, DOUBLE
       This type of plane was made to cut a symmetrical bevel on both sides of a door
       stile using the previously plowed panel groove as a guide. It is adjustable to
       match a groove ⅜ inches wide or wider. Adjustable door planes were listed
       by several American makers but were not illustrated. The plane shown was
       made by Edward Carter of Troy, N.Y.

No. 3R3 Door Plane, Double

3R3   DOOR PLANE, DOUBLE
       This double door plane will cut a round pattern moulding on both sides of a
       door stile or similar workpiece. It is adjustable to straddle a flat or groove of
       3/16 inches or greater. One side has a small extension to act as a guide for
       keeping the tool centered on the workpiece. It was made by Joseph Gibson of
       Albany, N.Y.

81

No. 3R4 Door Plane, Screw Arm

3R4   DOOR PLANE, SCREW ARM

This is another type of double door plane that will cut a bevel on both sides of a door stile with one pass of the plane. It uses the panel groove as a guide and is adjustable to fit grooves of various widths.

The plane was made by Ohio Tool Company and is marked No. 139½. This is a bevel pattern as can be seen in the illustration. The same type tool was also made with an ogee pattern instead of a bevel.

1877 (Ref. 9)

No. 3S1 Whip Plane

3S1   WHIP PLANE

Also listed as a Whip Maker's Plane.

This tool is a small plane hardly distinguishable from a small smoothing plane. One supplier listed it with a steel face. Salaman (Ref. 36) notes that the whip plane was used to pare down the tapered canes to form the handle of a whip.

No. 3T1 Meeting Rail Plane

3T1   MEETING RAIL PLANE

This type of plane was listed by several suppliers but never illustrated. It was a special purpose tool whose function was to make the stepped cut where the two sashes of a double hung window seat together.

The illustrated plane has an adjustable fence on the bottom and has two irons. Maximum width of the cut is 1¼ inches. It is marked Gardner & Murdock, Greenstreet, Boston.

No. 3U1 Basket Shave

3U1   BASKET SHAVE

Length: 4½ inches
Iron Width: 1¼ inches

This plane is used to smooth and to pare down the willow skeins previously split with another tool. It has a fixed iron and the sole is adjusted by a thumbscrew to vary the distance between the iron and the sole. The plane is held in a vise or clamp and the skein is pulled through between the iron and the sole thus reducing the strip to a fixed thickness. Salaman (Ref. 36) indicates that this tool is used only on the thin strips utilized for making light baskets and binding.

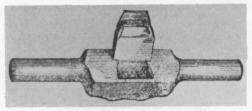

1877 (Ref. 9)

No. 3V1 Carriage Makers' Jarvis

3V1   CARRIAGE MAKERS' JARVIS
The jarvis is a two handed shave similar to a concave spoke shave except that the iron and throat are made similar to a bench plane. A jarvis is normally larger than a common shave and may be as much as 14 inches in length.

Sellens Collection

No. 3W1 Weatherstrip Planes, Pair

3W1   WEATHERSTRIP PLANES, PAIR
The illustrated pair of planes were bought for the purpose of installing the metal weatherstripping in double-hung window assemblies. One of the pair is a conventional ¾ inch square rabbet with a fixed metal fence let into one side. The other is a ⅛ inch grooving plane with an adjustable metal fence secured with thumbscrews. The grooving plane was used to plow a recess into each side of the sash for entry of the metal weatherstrip tongue. The owner was a little vague as to the exact purpose of the rabbet.

Both planes were made by Sandusky Tool Company and are marked "special" on the toe.

Rabbeting Planes

Numerical listing of rabbeting planes.

Ref. No.	Name
4A1	Rabbet Plane, Skew
4A2	Rabbet Plane, Square
4A3	Rabbet Plane, Handled
4A4	Rabbet Plane, Offset Handle
4A5	Rabbet Plane, Low Angle
4A6	Rabbet Plane, Circular
4A7	Rabbet Plane, Carriage Makers'
4A8	Rabbet Plane, Carriage Makers' T
4A9	Rabbet Plane, Carriage Makers' T
4A10	Rabbet Plane, Circular, Carriage
4A11	Rabbet Plane, Bridgebuilders
4A12	Rabbet Plane, Long
4B1	Filletster
4B2	Filletster, Side Stop
4B3	Filletster, Screw Stop
4B4	Filletster, Handled
4B5	Filletster, Wedge Arm
4B6	Filletster, Screw Arm
4B7	Filletster, Screw Arm, Handled
4B8	Sash Filletster, Wedge Arm
4B9	Sash Filletster, Screw Arm
4C1	Side Rabbet
4C2	Side Rabbet, Double
4D1	Halving Plane
4D2	Halving Plane, Handled

The wide variety of planes used for making or cleaning up a square bottomed groove in the edge of a workpiece are listed under the general heading of rabbeting planes. This type of cut is widely used in cabinet work, lap siding, window construction and numerous other areas.

Rabbets

The common rabbet plane is merely a square bottomed plane with the iron extending slightly more than full width of the sole. They were made in at least 18 different widths from ¼ inch to 2½ inches. The simplest types are similar to moulding planes in size: 9½ inches long and approximately 3½ inches deep. Larger sizes were available including some with handles.

An ordinary rabbet was unhandy to use because it required that a guide be clamped to the workpiece to control each cut. A fence was sometimes screwed or nailed to the side or sole of a rabbet to serve as a guide. Many of the old rabbet planes have several sets of screw holes where guides have been fastened. An occasional narrow rabbet is seen with 2 large holes thru the body. Such a plane used in conjunction with a pair of plow arms would serve the same purpose as a panel plow.

Rabbets could be bought with boxwood applied at the wear points to increase life. The illustration shows two examples of the application of boxwood.

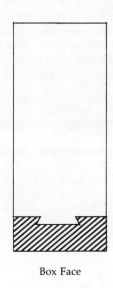

Box Corners   Box Face

1857 (Ref. 13)

Varieties of Rabbet Planes

Another optional feature on all varieties of rabbet planes was use of a spur or side cutter to score the cut ahead of the main iron. The purpose of a spur was to make a clean corner and avoid tearing the wood at the edge of the cut. Most sizes were available with either a single spur on the right side or with a spur on each side.

A handled rabbet with spurs on both sides has been called a banding plane by some writers. This type of rabbet was offered by most of the major American plane makers but none of them referred to the term Banding Plane in their sales literature.

By general definition, the purpose of a banding plane is to cut a flat bottomed groove in a curved surface. In order to accomplish such a cut, the spur cutters and the main iron would have to contact the workpiece at essentially the same point. Inasmuch as the spurs are set an inch or so ahead of the iron in a handled rabbet, it is concluded that a standard rabbet cannot be accurately labeled as a banding plane.

Whether to use the current American word Rabbet or the English spelling of the same word as Rebate has become a legitimate question inasmuch as some writers tend to use the two spellings interchangeably when referring to early planes and processes. A close review of all available American trade catalogs reveal that each catalog, without exception, used the American spelling or a slight variation. The 1858 Arrowmammett Catalog, Ref. 14, spelled the word as Rabbett and included "or Rebate" in parenthesis. The plane makers' listings provide adequate documentation that the term Rabbet had gained acceptance by American makers as early as the 1830s and was used from that point onward. The proper spelling to be used when referring to American planes is therefore considered to be Rabbet.

Sellens Collection

No. 4A1 Rabbet Plane, Skew

4A1   RABBET PLANE, SKEW
        Length: 9½ inches approximately
        Width of Cut: ¼, ⅜, ½, ⅝, ¾, ⅞, 1, 1⅛, 1¼, 1⅜, 1½, 1⅝, 1¾, 1⅞, 2, 2⅛,
            2¼, 2½ inches.
        Wood: Beech or boxwood.
        Available with one or two spurs.

        Some sizes were available with boxed corners, shoulder boxed or box faced.

        The skew rabbet shown in the illustration is 9½ inches long and 2 inches wide. It is marked A. Cumings, Boston.

No. 4A2 Rabbet Plane, Square

4A2 RABBET PLANE, SQUARE
Length: 9½ inches approximately
Width of Cut: ¼, ⅜, ½, ⅝, ¾, ⅞, 1, 1⅛, 1¼, 1½, 1¾, 2, 2⅛, 2¼ inches
Available with one or two spurs

Some sizes were available with boxed corners, shoulder boxed or boxed faced.

The rabbet shown in the illustration is 1⅝ inches wide and the standard 9½ inches long. It is marked C. Carter, Syracuse, N.Y.

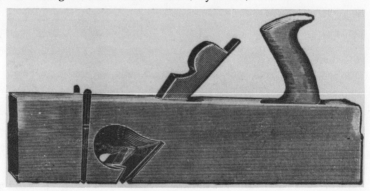

No. 4A3 Rabbet Plane, Handled   1901 (Ref. 1)

4A3 RABBET PLANE, HANDLED
Also called a Jack Rabbet or a Rabbet with Centre Handle. The term Jack Rabbet was applied because of the similarity in length and tote to the standard jack plane.
Length: 15 or 16 inches
Width of Cut: 1, 1¼, 1½, 1¾, 2, 2¼; 2½ inches
Skew set iron.

Available with either one or two spurs

Available with boxed corners or shoulder boxed.

88

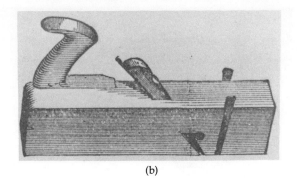

1877 (Ref. 9)

(b)

No. 4A4 Rabbet Plane, Offset Handle

4A4   RABBET PLANE, OFFSET HANDLE
Also called a Jack Rabbet
Length: 15 or 16 inches
Width of Iron: 1½, 1¾, 2, 2¼, 2½ inches
Skew set iron.

Available with either one or two spurs.

The offset type handle was particularly susceptible to breakage which partially accounts for the scarcity of these planes in good condition.

Sellens Collection

No. 4A5 Rabbet Plane, Low Angle

4A5   RABBET PLANE, LOW ANGLE
Length: 14 inches
Iron Width: 1 5/16
The illustrated skew rabbet has the appearance of a homemade tool but it is marked D. R. Barton on the toe. The rough surfaces and generally unfinished appearance are far below the quality standards of most Barton tools. Perhaps this was a special order item that was finished hurriedly. It is stamped 1½ on the heel and even that appears to be in error.

No. 4A6 Rabbet Plane, Circular

4A6   RABBET PLANE, CIRCULAR
Length: 9½ inches
The plane shown in the illustration has a ¾ inch iron. The screw holes in the side are evidence of repeated attachment of either a fence or a depth stop.

No. 4A7 Rabbet Plane, Carriage Makers'

4A7   RABBET PLANE, CARRIAGE MAKERS'
A carriage makers rabbet is essentially a smoothing plane with the sole cut away to expose the iron on both sides. Careful examination of most of these items will reveal that they are reworked smooth planes.

The illustrated plane is the less-common horn type with straight sides rather than the oval shape of the common smooth plane.

(a)   Marion Henley Collection

(b)   1880 (Ref. 15)

No. 4A8 Rabbet Plane, Carriage Makers' T

4A8   RABBET PLANE, CARRIAGE MAKERS' T
Also called a Carriage Makers' T Plane or a Coachmakers' T Plane

Several catalogs list this tool but none provide any mention of size. The plane shown in illustration (a) is 6 inches long and has a 1½ inch iron. It is marked I. Hammond, New Haven.

No. 4A9 Rabbet Plane, Carriage Makers' T

4A9   RABBET PLANE, CARRIAGE MAKERS' T
The illustration shows another excellent example of a T Rabbet. This type has the sole slightly curved in the side-to-side direction. It is 7 inches long and has a 1½ inch iron. This tool was made by Edward Carter of Troy.

Roger K. Smith Collection

No. 4A10 Rabbet Plane, Circular, Carriage

4A10   RABBET PLANE, CIRCULAR, CARRIAGE
Length: 6½ inches
Width of Iron: 1 inch
This little plane is marked Andruss.

Carriage maker's planes are always shorter than general purpose planes of a corresponding type presumedly to allow their use in fashioning the curved sections and curved decorations of a carriage.

No. 4A11 Rabbet Plane, Bridgebuilders'

4A11   RABBET PLANE, BRIDGEBUILDERS'
Also called a Ship Carpenters' Rabbet.
Length: 20 to 30 inches
Iron Width: 2 to 3 inches
These planes were available with either one or two side spurs. The illustrated
plane is 24 inches long and has a 3 inch iron.

No. 4A12 Rabbet Plane, Long

4A12   RABBET PLANE, LONG
Commercially made rabbets up to 24 inches long have been noted in tool
collection but those longer than the standard 9½ inches are scarce. The
illustrated plane is 15 inches long and was made by J. R. Tolman. Tolman was
known to have been a maker of ship building tools. This particular tool has a
double iron which is another feature that is quite scarce in a rabbet plane.

Filletsters

The common filletster, also called fillister and filister, serves the same purpose as a rabbet except that the filletster is always equipped with a fence. A more positive distinguishing feature is that a filletster has a mouth like a moulding plane which is quite different from the mouth of a rabbet. Early references to Standing and Moving filletsters indicate that they were made at one time with both fixed and adjustable fences. Apparently the standing filletsters went out of style and were not offered by most of the American planemakers. The catalogs generally listed filletsters but rarely mentioned the term Moving and did not even bother to state that they were adjustable. In keeping with the terminology of the American planemakers' lists, the filletsters listed herein have adjustable fences.

Common type filletsters have irons of 1¼ to 1⅝ inches wide. They were available with and without boxwood wear strips; however, most of those noted have at least a corner wear strip. Two types of boxwood application are shown in the illustration.

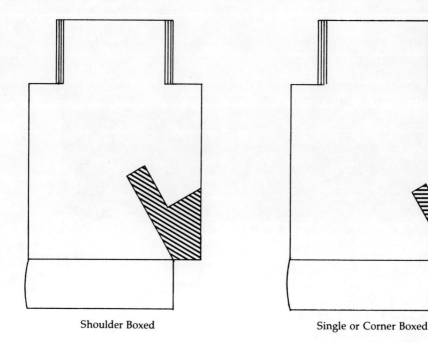

Shoulder Boxed   Single or Corner Boxed

Varieties of Filletsters

No. 4B1 Filletster

4B1   FILLETSTER
Also listed as a Plain Filletster
Length: 9½ inches approximately
This plain variety of filletster was available with or without a side spur.

The plane shown in the illustration is a Greenfield Tool Company No. 273. It is the standard 9½ inches long and has a 1⅝ inch iron. The mouth has been widened as can be seen in the photo.

(a)

1914 (Ref. 5)

No. 4B2 Filletster, Side Stop

Sellens Collection

No. 4B2 Filletster, Side Stop

4B2   FILLETSTER, SIDE STOP
Length: 9½ inches approximately
This type of filletster was available single boxed, solid boxed, shoulder boxed or plain. It was also available with or without a side cutter.

Illustration (b) shows a less common and probably older version of a side stop filletster having a slotted wooden stop.

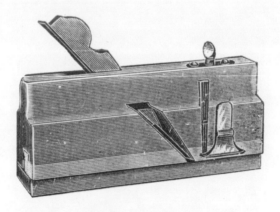

1914 (Ref. 5)

No. 4B3 Filletster, Screw Stop

4B3   FILLETSTER, SCREW STOP
This is the most common type of filletster.
Length: 9½ inches approximately
Wood Type: Beech, boxwood, rosewood or ebony
The beechwood planes were available with a boxwood fence. This variety of filletster was available with a boxed face or shoulder boxed. They could be bought with or without a side cutter.

96

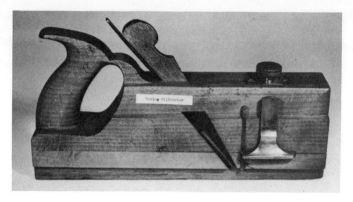

No. 4B4 Filletster, Handled

4B4 FILLETSTER, HANDLED
Wood Type: Beech, boxwood, rosewood or ebony
All of the handled filletsters noted in the catalogs were equipped with a side spur and a screw stop. They were available with either shoulder box or full box facing. One supplier listed this type of filletster as available with a rabbet mouth for a slight additional charge.

The plane illustrated is 11⅜ inches long and has a 1½ inch iron. It is marked Casey & Co., Auburn, N.Y.

No. 4B5 Filletster, Wedge Arm

4B5 FILLETSTER, WEDGE ARM
Sometimes listed as a Slide Arm Filletster.

Several suppliers offered filletsters with arms but none of the available catalogs contained an illustration or a description of the tool. Greenfield Tool Co. (Ref. 18), for example, offered both slide and screw arm filletsters with various features such as box strips and cutters.

The illustrated plane is a filletster equipped with plough-type arms. The single side cutter and single box strip show that it was made to cut on the right side only. The screw stop is identical to that used on a common filletster.

Length of the plane body is 9½ inches. It was made by T. G. M'Master & Co., Auburn, N.Y.

No. 4B6 Filletster, Screw Arm

4B6   FILLETSTER, SCREW ARM
This type of adjustable filletster was offered by several makers but seldom illustrated.

The plane shown is an Ohio Tool Co. No. 57. It was listed in the Ref. 5 catalog as a Boxed Screw Arm Filletster with Cutter. It has a spur cutter on both sides which allows it to double as a sash filletster.

Inasmuch as this plane has a rabbet mouth, it is probably the same tool that is listed as screw-arm rabbet by other suppliers.

No. 4B7 Filletster, Screw Arm, Handled

4B7   FILLETSTER, SCREW ARM, HANDLED

The illustrated plane is an Ohio Tool Company No. 58. It is listed in the company catalog as a "Fillister, with Cutter, Screw Stop, Screw Arms, Boxed, with Handle." This is the most expensive type of filletster offered by Ohio Tool.

No. 4B8 Sash Filletster, Wedge Arm

4B8   SASH FILLETSTER, WEDGE ARM
Also called a Back Filletster

This adjustable plane cuts the rabbet in a window sash using the opposite side of the sash bar as a guide. The iron is set to cut on the side adjacent to the fence which is opposite to the iron position on common filletsters. Note the boxwood wear strips inserted into the shoulder adjacent to the fence. The fence on a sash filletster is set much higher than on a common filletster because there is no need for the fence to slide underneath the cutting iron.

No. 4B9 Sash Filletster, Screw Arm

4B9   SASH FILLETSTER, SCREW ARM
The illustrated plane might also be called a screw arm rabbet combined with a
sash filletster. The two spur cutters and the two depth stops makes it equally
suitable for cutting on either side of the plane body.

100

No. 4C1 Side Rabbets

4C1   SIDE RABBETS
These tools were made to cut on the side only and intended to clean up the
side of a rabbet cut. They were sold in pairs consisting of one each to make RH
and LH cuts.
Length: 9½ inches approximately
The planes illustrated are a pair of No. 26 side rabbets made by D. R. Barton,
Rochester, N.Y.

No. 4C2 Side Rabbet, Double

4C2   SIDE RABBET, DOUBLE
       This unique plane has the general appearance of a homemade corebox plane
       but is equipped with a ½ inch cutting edge exposed on one side only of the
       right angle plane body. It would do a credible job of cleaning out the corner of
       a long wide rabbet but that task would hardly warrant the use of such a
       complicated tool. It is called a side rabbet for lack of a better name. The plane
       was made by Edward Carter of Troy, N.Y. and is 13 inches long.

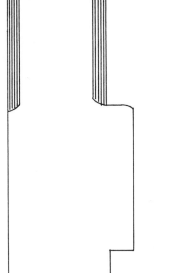

1872 (Ref. 18)

No. 4D1 Halving Plane

4D1   HALVING PLANE
Length: 9½ inches approximately
This type of plane is quite scarce and is rarely seen even in extensive tool collections. It was listed by several major suppliers but seldom illustrated. The plane shown is the standard 9½ inches long and was apparently made to cut a ⅜ x ⅜ rabbet in a ¾ inch workpiece. It is marked S. & H. Hills, Springfield, Mass. The advantages of the tool for making a specific sized rabbet are apparent in that the shape of the tool provides both a guide and a stop without need for measurements or adjustments.

No. 4D2 Halving Plane, Handled

4D2   HALVING PLANE, HANDLED
Length: 10½ inches
Size: Will cut a ½ x ½ inch rabbet
The illustrated plane has a plated fence and a skew set iron. The makers mark is C. B. Merthew.

Grooving Planes

Numerical listing of grooving planes.

Ref. No.	Name
5A1	Panel Plow, Screw Arm
5A2	Panel Plow, Handled
5A3	Panel Plow, Wood Stop
5A4	Panel Plow, Wedge Arm
5A5	Panel Plow, Slide Arm
5A6	Panel Plow, Center Screw
5A7	Panel Plow, Curved
5B1	Dado, Side Stop
5B2	Dado, Screw Stop
5B3	Dado, Wood Stop
5C1	Match Planes
5C2	Match Planes, Handled
5C3	Match Planes, Moving Fence
5C4	Match Planes, Plank
5C5	Match Plane, Combination
5C6	Match Plane, Combination
5C7	Match Plane, Combination, Handled
5C8	Match Planes, Screw Arm
5C9	Match Planes, Wedge Arm

The category of tools called grooving planes includes the panel plows for cutting grooves with the grain, dadoes for cutting across the grain and the broad family of match planes used for tongue and groove work.

The Panel Plow

The showpiece of the woodworkers tool box was the panel plow. It was also listed as a Grooving Plow or simply as a Plow Plane. The sole purpose of this fancy plane was to cut a narrow groove parallel with the edge of a workpiece and this cut could only be made with the grain. Much of the intricate design and trimming was for decoration only and are reminders of the pride of workmanship so often lacking in mass produced items. The plow was normally sold with eight irons as follows: 3/16, ¼, 5/16, ⅜, 7/16, ½, 9/16 and ⅝ inches. One supplier listed a ⅛ inch iron in lieu of the 9/16 inch. The less expensive types of plows were sometimes sold with only four irons and were listed without irons by one supplier. Ohio Tool Co. (Ref. 1) listed the handled plows with either a round handle or an improved handle for the right hand. No. 5A2 illustrations show the two types of handles.

American panel plows have the arms attached to the fence and adjust thru holes in the plane body. This is a feature copied from British planemakers. French and certain other Continental plows are generally made with the adjustment arms attached to the plane body such that they adjust through holes in the fence.

The several varieties of panel plows were listed by some suppliers in four different qualities called 1st rate, 2nd rate, etc. For example, the type with set-screw arms could be bought in four different price ranges. The first rate planes had a screw stop and were trimmed with brass ferrules on the arms while the 2nd rate items had a screw stop but not ferrules. The 3rd rate plane had a wood stop held with a wood set screw. A wood stop held only by friction was used on the 4th rate planes of this variety. Finish, workmanship and even the wood were of better quality on the higher rated plows.

These planes were made of beechwood except as noted on the individual description pages.

(a)   Sellens Collection

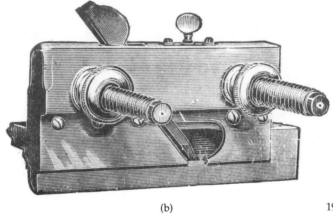

(b)   1901 (Ref. 1)

No. 5A1 Panel Plow, Screw Arm

5A1   PANEL PLOW, SCREW ARM
        The most common variety of panel plow had screw arm lateral adjustments
        and a screw type of depth stop.
        Length: 8 inch sole approximately
        Irons: Usually sold with 8 irons. Occasionally listed with 4 irons only.
        Wood Type: Beech, boxwood, apple, rosewood, ebony, beech with boxwood
            arms, beech with dogwood arms, apple with boxwood arms, rosewood
            with boxwood arms or beech with ironwood arms.
        This type plane was available with or without a boxwood wear strip on the
        fence.

        The screw stop was generally made of brass but iron stops were also used by
        some suppliers. A side screw to lock the stop was provided on the more
        expensive varieties. Metal plating of brass or iron was used by some suppliers
        and was an optional feature in other listings. Ivory trimming was popular on
        plow planes and several suppliers listed the better quality plows with and

without trimming. Ivory tips on the screw arms was the most common type of trim followed by ivory bands on the screw arm nuts.

The plane shown in illustration (a) is made of solid boxwood including the arms and fence. It is marked Child.Pratt & Co., St. Louis, Mo.

(a)   Sellens Collection

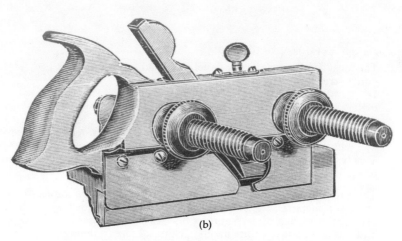

(b)

No. 5A2 Panel Plow, Handled   1901 (Ref. 1)

108

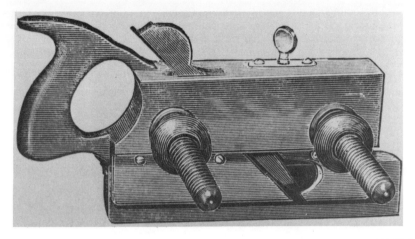

(c)   1901 (Ref. 1)

(d)   George Tuttle Collection

No. 5A2 Panel Plow, Handled

5A2   PANEL PLOW, HANDLED
    Length: 11 inches overall and approximately an 8 inch sole
    Irons: Usually sold with 8 irons but occasionally listed with 4 irons only
    Wood Type: Beech, boxwood, rosewood, apple, ebony, beech with boxwood
        arms, apple with boxwood arms or rosewood with boxwood arms.
    These planes were available with and without boxwood wear strips on the
    fence. Either iron or brass screw stops were available and some varieties had a
    brass side screw to lock the depth stop. Metal plating of brass or iron was used
    by some suppliers and was an optional feature in other listings. Ivory tips on
    the screw arms and ivory bands on the knobs were available at extra cost. One
    supplier listed the most expensive plow as being silver mounted and another
    listing included silver plated facings.

109

The distinctive plow shown in illustration (d) was made by E. W. Carpenter of Lancaster, Pa. Brass fittings are used to attach the handle and to improve the appearance of the tool. Like most of the planes made by Carpenter, this plow shows an added measure of quality in both design and workmanship.

The plane shown in illustration (a) is marked No. 124, A.C. Bartletts Ohio Planes. It has a right handed handle and a boxed fence. The boxwood strip is dovetailed to the fence.

Sellens Collection

No. 5A3 Panel Plow, Wood Stop

5A3   PANEL PLOW, WOOD STOP
The least expensive of the screw arm plows was equipped with a wood stop in lieu of the brass screw stop. A wood set screw was normally used to prevent movement of the stop.
Length: 8 inch sole approximately
Irons: Normally sold with 8 irons but occasionally listed with only 4
These planes were available with and without boxwood wear strips on the fence.

The illustrated plane is a standard size beechwood plow made by Pratt & Co., Buffalo. The stop and set screw are made of boxwood.

George Tuttle Collection

No. 5A4 Panel Plow, Wedge Arms

5A4   PANEL PLOW, WEDGE ARMS
       Also listed as a Slide Arm Plow
       Length: 8 inch sole approximately
       Irons: Usually sold with 8 irons but occasionally listed with only 4
       Wood type: Beech or boxwood
       This type of plow was available with or without boxwood wear strips on the
       fence and brass plating on the main body.

       The illustrated plane was made by A. & E. Baldwin. The brass ferrules on
       each end of the arms was an optional feature available on this type of plow.

1872 (Ref. 18)

Sellens Collection

No. 5A5 Panel Plow, Slide Arm

5A5   PANEL PLOW, SLIDE ARM
       Length: 8 inch sole approximately
       Irons: Usually sold with 8 irons but occasionally listed with only 4
       These planes were available with and without boxwood wear strips and with
       or without plating. They were listed with either the standard screw stop or
       with a boxwood stop similar to the Wood Stop Plow previously discussed.

       The illustrated plane is an example of the third rate variety of panel plows. It
       is neither boxed nor plated. The arms are riveted to the fence thus avoiding
       the use of 2 screws.

111

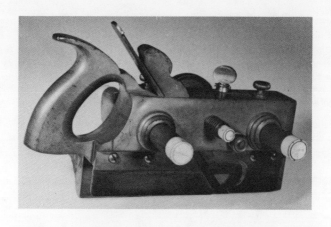

No. 5A6 Panel Plow, Center Screw

5A6   PANEL PLOW, CENTER SCREW
       Also called a Side Wheel Plow.

The fancy Sandusky Tool Co. panel plow shown in the illustrations is an
attempt to improve on the basic plow design. Rigidity between the fence and
the main body are doubtlessly improved and perhaps it is easier to attain
proper alignment of the fence. It appears that the greatest improvement lies
in the decorative effect of using more brass and ivory. The brass center wheel
and six ivory tips make this plane a true showpiece.

No. 5A7 Panel Plow, Curved

5A7 PANEL PLOW, CURVED

This unique panel plow was designed to plow a groove in a curved work-piece. The body is 6⅜ inches long which is only slightly shorter than the standard plow, however the sole is only three inches long as can be seen in the illustration. The fence has a flexible steel facing that can be adjusted to match the contour being plowed.

113

The Dado

Cutting a square bottomed groove across the grain is a task for a dado plane. Unlike the plow, the dado has a vertical iron to score the edges of the cut ahead of the main iron. The feature allows cross grain cutting without tearing the edges of the cut. The iron is always skewed to further aid in achieving a clean cross-grain cut. Dadoes were made in several patterns and in at least 12 different widths.

A little used name for the dado was Cut Thrust or Cut and Thrust.

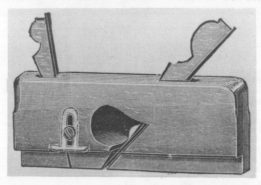

1914 (Ref. 5)

No. 5B1 Dado, Side Stop

5B1   DADO, SIDE STOP
Length: 9½ inches approximately
Width of Iron: ⅛, 3/16, ¼, 5/16, ⅜, ½, ⅝, ¾, ⅞, 1, 1⅛, 1¼ inches
The side stop was generally made of brass but some makers also offered an iron stop.

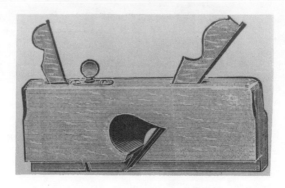

1914 (Ref. 5)

No. 5B2 Dado, Screw Stop

5B2   DADO, SCREW STOP
Length: 9½ inches approximately
Width of Iron: ⅛, 3/16, ¼, 5/16, ⅜, ½, ⅝, ¾, ⅞, 1, 1⅛, 1¼ inches

No. 5B3 Dado, Wood Stop

5B3 DADO, WOOD STOP
Length: 9½ inches approximately
Width of Iron: ⅛, 3/16, ¼, 5/16, ⅜, ½, ⅝, ¾, ⅞, 1, 1⅛, 1¼ inches
The stop was generally specified as boxwood.

Wood stop dadoes were made with and without a set screw to hold the stop in place. When a set screw was not used, the stop was made to a precision fit such that friction would prevent movement during use. It is reasonable to assume that these friction-held slides would tend to become loose with usage and with shrinkage of the wood. Perhaps this is why many of the plane suppliers did not offer the wood stop variety of dado.

The plane shown in the illustration is a ¾ inch dado marked T. J. M'Master & Co., Auburn. A wood set screw is used to secure the stop.

Match Planes

The planes used to make the matching tongues and grooves for edge joining are called match planes. These tools were made in a wide variety of sizes and shapes the most common of which was the nonadjustable 9½ board match set. Match planes were normally sold in pairs, one plane would cut the groove and the other plane would make the matching tongue. Fixed sizes were made to work 9 different stock thicknesses from ¼ to 1½ inches. In addition to the fixed sizes, several varieties of adjustable match sets were available. The better quality of sets had metal rub-plates along the shoulder of each plane to avoid error due to wear. Planes with the metal strips were said to be plated or faced.

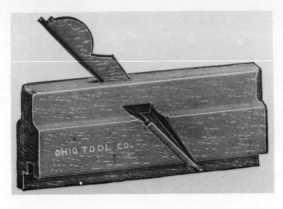

1914 (Ref. 5)

No. 5C1 Match Planes

5C1   MATCH PLANES
Also called Board Match Planes
Length: 9½ inches approximately
Size: For ¼, ⅜, ½, ⅝, ¾, ⅞, 1, 1¼, 1½ inch stock thickness.
These planes were available with and without plating.

The ¼ inch size planes were not offered by all suppliers and are quite scarce.

No. 5C2 Match Planes, Handled

5C2 MATCH PLANES, HANDLED
Also called Board Match Planes
Length: 11½ inches appróximately
Size: For ¼, ⅜, ½, ⅝, ¾, ⅞, 1, 1¼, 1½ inch stock thickness
Wood type: Beech or apple
These planes were sold with and without plating. Some makers referred to
Faced Planes instead of Plated Planes.

The handled match set shown in the illustration is a matched pair of D. R.
Barton 1 inch full-plated planes. The reason for the hole in one of the planes is
unknown.

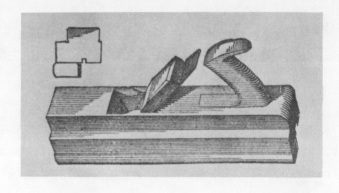

1877 (Ref. 9)

No. 5C3 Match Planes, Moving Fence

5C3   MATCH PLANES, MOVING FENCE
These planes have a movable fence attached to the sole with two recessed-head screws working in a slot in the same manner as the common filletster. They were available with and without plating.

118

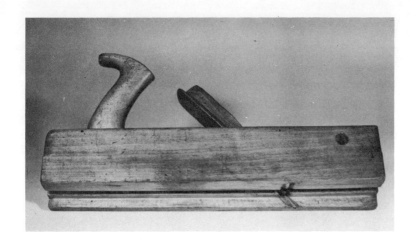

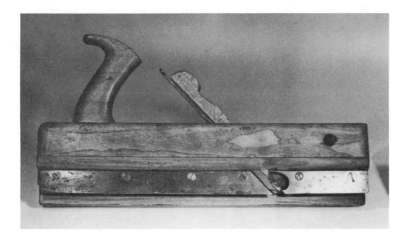

George Tuttle Collection

No. 5C4 Match Planes, Plank

5C4   MATCH PLANES, PLANK
Length: 14 to 15 inches
Size: For 1, 1¼, 1½, 2 inch stock thickness
These planes were available plated and with box strips.

The pair of plank match planes in the illustration are 14¼ inches long. They are marked G. King.

119

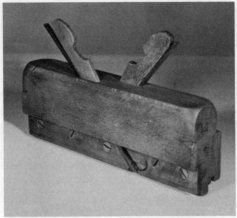

No. 5C5 Match Plane, Combination

5C5   MATCH PLANE, COMBINATION
Also called Double or Twin Match
Length: 9½ inches approximately
Size: For ¼, ⅜, ½, ⅝, ¾, ⅞, 1 inch stock thickness
These planes were available with and without plating.

The illustrated plane is a No. 75 marked Scioto Works. Scioto is a brand name used by Ohio Tool Co. on second grade tools. This plane is made to work ½ inch stock and cuts a groove about ⅛ inch wide.

No. 5C6 Match Plane, Combination

5C6   MATCH PLANE, COMBINATION
Length: 9½ inches
The unique feature of this plane is that the tonguing and grooving irons are set side by side rather than facing in opposite directions as in most combination match planes.

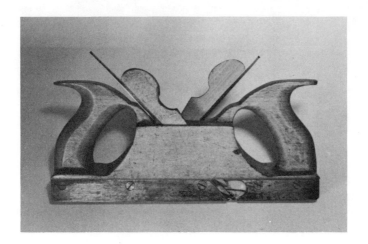

No. 5C7 Match Plane, Combination, Handled

5C7   MATCH PLANE, COMBINATION, HANDLED
      Length: 10¾ inches
      The illustrated plane was made by the Auburn Tool Co. It will cut a 3/16 inch
      groove.

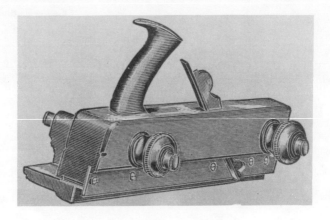

1914 (Ref. 5)

No. 5C8 Match Planes, Screw Arm

5C8 MATCH PLANES, SCREW ARM
     Also called Moving Match or Plank Match with Screw Arms
     Length: 13 to 15 inches
     Wood Type: Beech, boxwood, beech with applewood arms or beech with
         boxwood arms
     Also available plated and with boxed fence

No. 5C9 Match Planes, Wedge Arm

5C9   MATCH PLANES, WEDGE ARM
Length: 13 to 15 inches
The arms were tipped with brass ferrules on the more expensive varieties of wedge arm planes.

The pair of wedge arm match planes shown in the illustration were made by J. Harrison & Co. Length of the soles is 13¾ inches.

Simple Moulding Planes

Numerical listing of simple moulding planes.

Moulding Planes - General

The moulding plane family includes an extremely wide variety of tools used to create the intricate and decorative woodwork common in 19th century buildings. They were seldom, if ever, used for any utilitarian purpose. Despite their lack of utility, moulding planes were standard items in every finish carpenters tool box and in every cabinet shop. The term moulding plane normally is used to refer to the small single iron plane approximately 9½ inches long and 3½ inches deep. Other sizes were made in lesser quantities. The planes to strike wide mouldings were often made with handles and have been noted in various lengths up to 16 inches. The 9½ inch length apparently evolved as an unofficial standard among the English planemakers prior to the nineteenth century and this standard size was generally adopted by the American makers. The reasons for choosing that particular size are not known, however the 9½ inch length is small enough for convenient storage on a shelf or in a toolbox tray and yet large enough to be easily grasped with both hands. Manufacturers continued to make their planes similar to the existing types probably in an effort to sell single replacement planes for a set. There was no doubt a brisk replacement business for the common sizes that become worn or damaged.

Commercial manufacture of moulding planes started in the United States prior to 1800 and scores of makers were turning out planes by the middle of the nineteenth century. It is probable that the moulding plane industry reached its peak about the 1870 - 1880 time period. By this period, mill-cut mouldings were readily available in the industrial areas and transportation was becoming cheaper and more dependable. Invention and marketing of the metallic combination planes about this same time period also hastened the decline of wood-bodied moulding planes. A single combination plane was capable of making numerous types of cuts and was ideal for working a replacement moulding or for use on small jobs. A full line of wood bodied moulding planes were stock listed in 1900 - 1915 vintage hardware catalogs, however it is doubtful if many were sold at that time. By 1900, most of the small makers had ceased operation leaving the remaining business to only a few of the larger concerns such as Ohio Tool Company and Chapin-Stevens Company.

As evidence that wood-bodied moulding planes were not entirely obsoleted by the combination planes, the following editorial comment is quoted from a Tool Catalog published by Chas. A. Strelinger & Co., Detroit, Mich. dated 1897: "While to a great extent the Combination Planes like the No. 45 are taking the place of the Moulding Planes, they do not by any means cover the entire ground. Where a considerable quantity of a certain kind of work is to be done, the Wood Planes are so much lighter and so much more convenient to handle, that it is not always the best economy to use a Combination Plane for this class of work."

The moulding planes shown herein were all made of beechwood. Early American planemakers often made moulding planes of birch and an occasional one has been noted to be made of apple or cherry. A careful review of catalog data has failed to reveal a single listing of moulding planes made of any wood other than beech. It seems safe to conclude that the use of beechwood for this purpose became almost universal after the 1840-50 time period.

Many moulding planes have a line scribed on the toe to assist the user in establishing and maintaining a proper angle with the workpiece. In practice, the scribe line was held vertical to the workpiece thus obtaining the correct canted position of the tool. These lines were added by the owner and user of the plane rather than by the supplier.

A short review of some of the names of the mouldings and terminology associated with wooden moulding planes is provided to establish a common base for discussion. It should be kept in mind that mouldings of the Roman influence are formed primarily from sections of the arc of a circle while Grecian mouldings are formed from conic sections or portions of an ellipse or cycloid. The Roman mouldings therefore appear as vigorous or abrupt curves when compared to the flatter and more graceful curves of the Grecian mouldings. In addition, the Grecian mouldings are often quirked in at the extreme top to emphasize shadow.

QUIRK

Sometimes abbreviated Qk in the plane catalogs.

A quirk is usually defined as a sudden turn in curvature or as a small acute angle between mouldings or portions of a moulding. Reference 28 offers the following definition:

Quirk-moulding — One whose sharp and sudden return from its extreme projection to the reentrant angle seems rather to partake of a straight line on the profile than of the curve.

BEAD

Knight (Ref. 26) defines Bead as "A small salient moulding of semicircular section." This simple definition becomes somewhat obscured by the names applied to the various varieties of beads. The moulding plane listed by some suppliers as a bead is the same as a side bead listed in other catalogs. The astragal is also a bead hardly distinguishable from the common bead and the torus is generally defined by the dictionaries as the same as an astragal only larger. Fortunately the plane suppliers provided detail contour drawings in their catalogs to define several varieties of beads at least from the plane makers standpoint. These contours are included under the individual plane headings. It is noted that the American planemakers definitions do not necessarily agree with the common encyclopedia definitions. Any attempt at general comparison of the two descriptions only results in complication.

OVOLO

This is the moulding plane contour most easily mistaken. The catalogs are not helpful in dispelling the misunderstandings caused by the several names applied to an ovolo. Actually, an ovolo can be either of two types of curves as shown in the following illustrations.

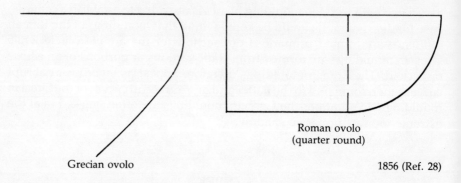

Grecian ovolo

Roman ovolo
(quarter round)

1856 (Ref. 28)

Discussion is made somewhat clearer by referring to the Roman influenced ovolo as a quarter round as did most plane suppliers.

OGEE

The S shaped double curve called the Ogee is the moulding contour most used in the era of American wooden planes. The two curves illustrated are characteristic ogee contours.

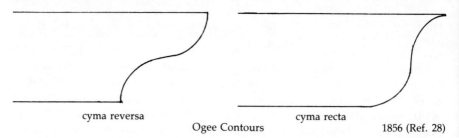

cyma reversa

cyma recta

Ogee Contours

1856 (Ref. 28)

The ogee curve of the Roman influence tends to be sharper and more abrupt than the Grecian variety.

SCOTIA AND COVE

The plane suppliers catalogs tend to use Cove and Scotia as interchangeable terms. The Carpenters Assistant again illustrated them both for ready comparison as shown in the illustration. The Cove was also known as a Cavetto.

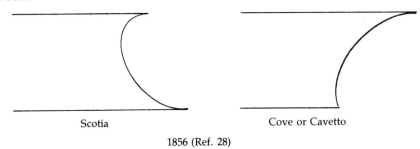

| Scotia | Cove or Cavetto |

1856 (Ref. 28)

Fillet - a small rectangular projection at one extreme edge of a moulding. A small square projection beyond the moulding.

Bevel - A small inclined projection at one extreme edge of a moulding. A bevel was occasionally listed as a Splay.

Some common types of moulding planes are listed and illustrated on the following pages. Only the more common types are illustrated, however these few types encompass the vast majority of moulding planes in terms of quantity extant. Practically every supplier offered a complete line of the several common types such as the cove, side bead and grecian ogee. Several of the major makers also offered to make moulding planes to any desired pattern but noted the extra cost and necessary delay in delivery. This practice of making planes on special order accounts for the seemingly endless variety of moulding planes.

The term "Moulding Plane" is used in this volume because most of the American makers used this term and this spelling to describe the product. The terms Moulding Tool, Molding Tool and Molding Plane were also used to a lesser degree and should not be considered as inaccurate.

For purposes of discussion, moulding planes are arbitrarily divided into two groupings called Simple and Complex. Division is in general agreement with the definition made in the December 1967 Issue of *Chronicle* (Ref. 24). As defined in the Chronicle, a simple moulding is formed primarily by a portion of an arc of a circle and a complex moulding is one having two or more intersecting curves. It should be remembered that these terms are used for convenience only and were not used by the makers and craftsmen.

129

Simple Moulding Planes

A simple moulding plane is one in which the moulding contour is formed primarily by a single portion of an arc. This rather narrow definition covers a considerable percentage of the moulding planes extant. Included in this category are the hollows and rounds, quarter rounds, coves and the various single beads. Reeding and multiple reeding planes are included because they are merely extended versions of the center bead. The snipe bill is included in this listing because it cuts a single surface. Like the hollow and round, the snipe bill is not intended to be a complete moulding tool. Each is used in conjunction with other planes to create the desired moulding contour or to clean up a moulding made by another plane.

Unless otherwise noted under the individual descriptions, each of the simple moulding planes is the standard length of approximately 9½ inches, and has a single iron.

 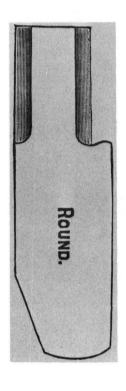

1914 (Ref. 5)

No. 6A1 Hollow and Round Pair

131

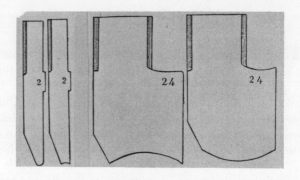

1872 (Ref. 18)

No. 6A1 Hollow and Round Pair

6A1   HOLLOW AND ROUND PAIR
Most common of the moulding planes are the simple hollow and round pairs. The hollow has a concave face (hollow) as shown in the sketch and the round has a convex surface. These planes were used with other types of moulding planes or with other sizes of hollows and rounds to produce various moulding contours. They were also useful in cutting a simple curve for any number of purposes such as on a porch rail or an implement handle and could be used efficiently to hollow out a trough or an open pipe.
Size: Available in 32 sizes from 1/16 to 2 inches wide
A number denoting the size is marked in the heel for easy reading when the plane is setting on the shelf. The size numbering refers to iron width but the numbering schemes appear to have been established to confound the scholar and to confuse the collector. Numbers from 1 upward were assigned by each maker to denote increasing iron widths. The three prominent numbering schemes consisted of sizes from 1 to 15, 1 to 24 and 1 to 30 with each scheme apparently covering widths up to 2 inches. However, variations within each scheme are sufficient to disprove any general rule. For instance, Barton's catalog (Ref. 9) lists numbers 1 thru 12 and 14 thru 18, leading one to believe that odd sizes above 12 were not available. No sooner was this rule established than a number 17 turned up in an old tool box. Another confusing factor is two Number 7 Ohio Tool Co. Model 72 hollows which are different sizes. It is speculated that this was a simple numbering error or was the result of filling a replacement order for a company absorbed by Ohio Tool. Regardless of the cause, it is illustrative of the fact that even a set from a given maker may not be free of incongruities. Inasmuch as some suppliers stated that smaller, intermediate and larger size pieces were available on request, certain anomalies can be credited to special order items. The authors collection includes a 2¾ inch round made by P. Brooks that is clearly marked 2¼ on the heel.

Hollows and rounds were normally sold by the matched pair or in sets of nine, ten or twelve pairs. Nine pairs was the set most commonly quoted. One company listed individual planes in addition to pairs but this was not a normal practice with most suppliers.

132

A set of nine pairs offered by one maker or jobber did not necessarily consist of the same sizes as a set from another supplier. For example a set of 9 pairs from the 1897 Sears catalog would include ¼ to 1½ inch widths and a set from Ohio Tool Co. would include ¼ to 1¼ inch widths. It is not known why nine pairs became known as a set. Eighteen planes of one type would seem to be an excessive number for the average journeyman to store and to transport from one job to another. It has been observed that most old tool boxes contain from 3 to 6 pairs rather than 9. The sets of 9 or more pairs were apparently sold to the cabinet or other woodworking shops. A "complete set" of hollows and rounds could consist of one pair bought by an apprentice carpenter, four pairs owned by a journeyman or as many as 60 pairs (straight plus skew) owned by a large shop. In other words, a complete set from a users standpoint is however many he thinks is necessary for his job.

Hollow and round irons were formed to span approximately 60 degrees of arc or 1/6 of a circle. The word approximate is used because it is known that some makers did not use this exact contour. Variations between used planes could be the result of wear or sharpening, however two distinct patterns are noted in the Ohio Tool Co. 1914 catalog. This catalog states that the Ohio pattern 2 inch iron, for instance works a 4 inch circle (60 degrees of arc) while an Auburn pattern works a 4½ inch circle. Apparently the Ohio Tool Co. continued to make hollows and rounds in both patterns after absorbing Auburn Tool.

The illustration shows an end view of a large and small pair. This general shape was used by most if not all suppliers. The Ref. 5 illustration is included to clearly show which plane should be called a hollow and which should be called a round. The nomenclature has long been a confusing point inasmuch as most moulding planes are labeled for the type of curve that they cut rather than for the shape of the sole. For instance, a quarter round plane cuts a quarter round moulding which is of course opposite from its concave sole. Conversly, a hollow plane actually has a hollow or concave sole and is not labeled for the type of curve that it cuts.

Sellens Collection

No. 6A2 Hollow and Round Pair, Skew

6A2 HOLLOW AND ROUND PAIR, SKEW

Hollow and Round pairs with skew set irons were listed by several suppliers in the same sizes as the regular straight set hollows and rounds. For reasons yet to be explained, these skew planes are quite scarce. The most probable reason for the scarcity is that the skew type planes cost 20 to 25 percent more than the common straight type.

Size: Same as the No. 6A1 Hollow and Round Pair.

The pair shown in the illustration were made by Ohio Tool Co. and are marked with a series number of 72½. They are size 9.

Fred Bair Collection

No. 6A3 Side Round Pair

6A3 SIDE ROUND PAIR

This pair of planes were designed for making right and left hand cuts using the side of the tool. American made planes of this type are scarce. The illustrated planes are marked No. 8 on the heel. It is probable that they were made in all sizes to correspond with the standard hollow and round pairs.

Sellens Collection

No. 6A4 Ship Hollow and Round Pair

134

6A4 SHIP HOLLOW AND ROUND PAIR

Hollows and rounds with a bench mouth are commonly called ship planes in the New England area. They are generally made for double irons and are slightly thicker in the center giving them an oval shape as can be seen in the illustration. Sizes noted are from ¾ to 1½ inches.

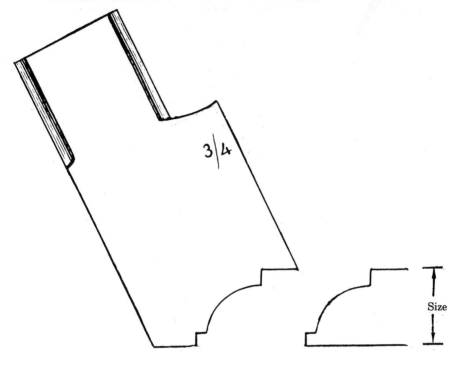

3|4

Size

1857 (Ref. 13)

No. 6B1 Quarter Round

6B1 QUARTER ROUND

This type of plane was called a Plain Ovolo by one maker and a Scotia by certain other makers. An Ovolo of Roman character can be defined as a simple quarter arc of a circle; however, an ovolo moulding is generally made with a somewhat flat unsymmetrical curve rather than a true arc. A Scotia moulding is defined by the reference encyclopedias as having an unsymmetrical concave shape.

Neither the quarter round plane nor the moulding it produces bears a reasonable resemblance to an architectural scotia. The term scotia is further perverted in that several suppliers refer to a cove moulding as a scotia. It is concluded that use of either the term Plain Ovolo or Scotia in defining this plane could only lead to more confusion. Although the term Ovolo is technically correct, Quarter Round is considered to be the preferred name.

Size: Size in inches is normally stamped on the heel. The following ten sizes were offered: ¼, ⅜, ½, ⅝, ¾, ⅞, 1, 1¼, 1⅜, 1½ inches.

The size refers to the height of the cut as shown in the illustration.

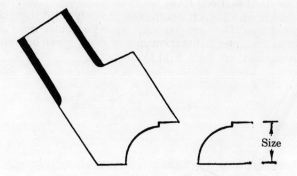

No. 6B2 Casing Moulding

6B2   CASING MOULDING
Also listed as a Quarter Round.

These planes were tools of the finish carpenter as well as cabinet maker. The casing moulding was used in a variety of applications where relief from a square juncture was needed. This pattern was popular for making door and window casings.

Size: Size in inches is normally stamped on the heel. The following eight sizes were offered: ⅜, ½, ⅝, ¾, ⅞, 1, 1¼, 1½ inches

The size refers to the thickness of stock to be worked as shown in the illustration.

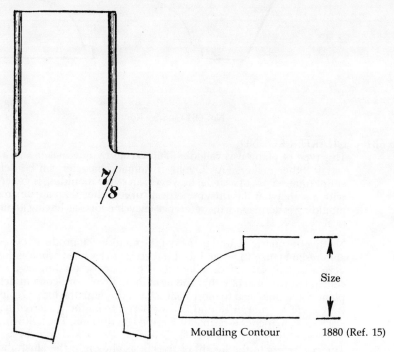

Moulding Contour   1880 (Ref. 15)

No. 6B3 Casing Moulding with Fence

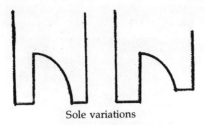

Sole variations

6B3 CASING MOULDING WITH FENCE
Also listed as Quarter Round and Quarter Round with Fence.
Size: Size in inches is normally stamped on the heel. The following nine
sizes were offered: ¼, ⅜, ½, ⅝, ¾, ⅞, 1, 1¼, 1½ inches
The size refers to the thickness of stock to be worked as shown in the
illustration.

The Ref. 1 Catalog of 1901 referred to this casing plane as a new type that is
easier to work.

W.L. Gordon Collection

No. 6B4 Casing Moulding, Curved

6B4 CASING MOULDING, CURVED
This unique curved moulding plane is 7½ inches long and has a 1-9/16 inch
double iron. The maker is A. Cumings of Boston. Cumings made planes in
Boston about 1850 and is known to have made many special purpose tools.
This plane could have been used by a ship fitter or possibly a stair builder.

137

No. 6B5 Casing Moulding, Handled

6B5   CASING MOULDING, HANDLED
Available catalogues and broadsides do not list casing moulding planes with handles. The illustrated tool was probably a special order item by a craftsman who wanted to maintain more precise control of the tool or by one who intended to use it extensively.

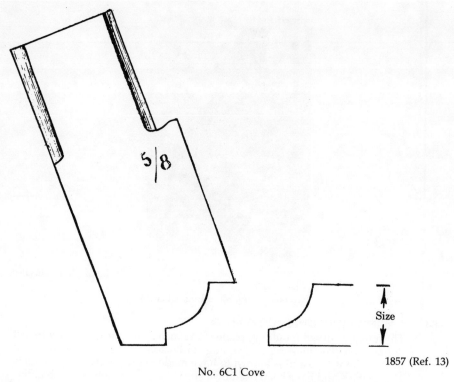

5|8

Size

1857 (Ref. 13)

No. 6C1 Cove

138

6C1 COVE

This type of plane is often listed as a Stair Cove or as a Scotia. The moulding contour that it cuts bears a resemblance to a scotia in that it is concave, however a scotia is normally defined as an unsymmetrical concave shape. Inasmuch as the Quarter Round moulding plane was also listed as a Scotia, (see No. 6B1) the term cove is considered to be more definitive for this type of tool.

Sizes: The size in inches is normally stamped on the heel. The following nine
          sizes were offered: ¼, ⅜, ½, ⅝, ¾, ⅞, 1, 1¼, 1½ inches

The size number usually refers to the thickness of stock to be worked but in some cases the actual depth of the moulding contour is used as the size.

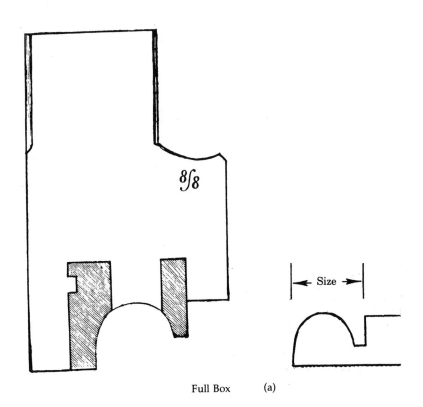

Full Box   (a)

No. 6D1 Side Bead

139

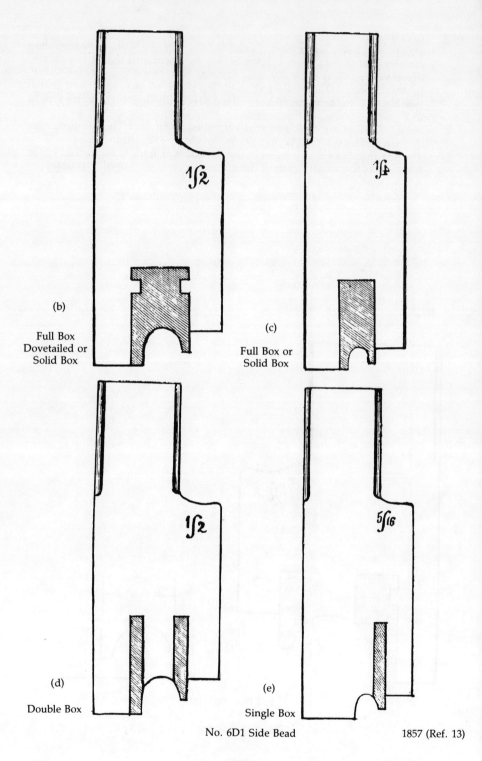

(b)

Full Box
Dovetailed or
Solid Box

(c)

Full Box or
Solid Box

(d)

Double Box

(e)

Single Box

No. 6D1 Side Bead

1857 (Ref. 13)

6D1   SIDE BEAD
       Also listed merely as a Bead

The side bead was used to make a decorative bead along the edge of a workpiece. The shape of the cut moulding is shown in the illustration.

Size: Size in inches is normally stamped on the heel. The following 18 sizes were offered: 1/8, 3/16, 1/4, 5/16, 3/8, 7/16, 1/2, 9/16, 5/8, 3/4, 7/8, 1, 1 1/8, 1 1/4, 1 3/8, 1 1/2, 1 3/4, 2 inches

The full line of sizes was available single boxed, double boxed or solid boxed.

The size number stamped on the heel refers to the width of cut including the groove.

All side bead planes noted in the commercial listings were faced with boxwood strips at one or more wear points to prolong life of the tool. They were said to be single boxed, double boxed or full (solid) boxed depending upon the type of wear strips provided. The various types of boxing are shown in the rear view illustrations (b) thru (e). The full box type using 2 strips of boxwood, as shown in illustration (a), was used for large sizes only.

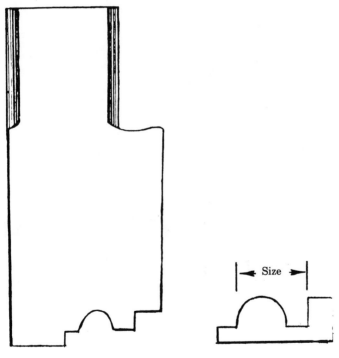

Size

1857 (Ref. 13)

No. 6D2 Astragal

6D2   ASTRAGAL
       Also spelled Astrigal and Ostrigal in some catalogs

This plane forms a contour similar to the side bead moulding plane except that the bead is set back a fixed distance from the edge of the work piece as shown in the illustration.

Size: Size in inches is normally stamped on the heel. The following 14 sizes were offered: ⅛, 3/16, ¼, 5/16, ⅜, ½, ⅝, ¾, ⅞, 1, 1⅛, 1¼, 1⅜, 1½ inches

The size refers to the width of the bead plus the groove as shown in the illustration. This size definition was ascertained by measurement of actual planes.

Boxwood strips were sometimes inserted at the wear points to increase the life of the tool.

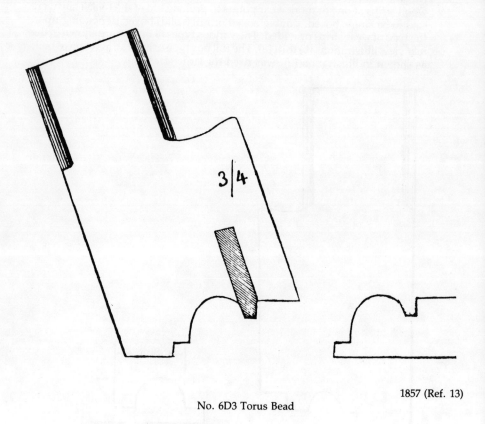

3|4

1857 (Ref. 13)

No. 6D3 Torus Bead

6D3   TORUS BEAD

The torus bead is used to cut an edge design similar to that made by an astragal.

Size: The size in inches is normally stamped on the heel. The following nine sizes were offered: ¼, ⅜, ½, ⅝, ¾, ⅞, 1, 1¼, 1½ inches

The size refers to the width of the groove plus the width of the bead as shown in the astragal moulding plane illustration.

No. 6D4 Double Side Bead

6D4   DOUBLE SIDE BEAD
Also listed as Twin Bead and as a Double Bead.

This plane is actually a right and left side bead constructed from one piece of wood. The moulding contour is the same as that made by a conventional side bead.
Size: The size in inches is normally stamped on the heel. The following thirteen sizes were offered: ⅛, 3/16, ¼, 5/16, ⅜, ½, 9/16, ⅝, ¾, ⅞, 1, 1⅛, 1¼ inches
The plane shown in the illustration was made by M. Copeland. Both beads are size ⅜ inch.

No. 6D5 Side Bead, Curved

6D5   SIDE BEAD, CURVED
Length: 7 Inches
Size: ¼ inch
The illustrated plane was probably a coachmakers tool but may have been used by a ship fitter or any other craftsman needing a curved moulding.

143

Donald Wing Collection

No. 6D6 Side Bead, Handled

6D6   SIDE BEAD, HANDLED

This scarce variety of side bead has a jack type razee handle and two irons.
Available catalogs do not list handled side beads.

Roger K. Smith Collection

Sellens Collection

No. 6D7 Side Bead, Double Iron

6D7 SIDE BEAD, DOUBLE IRON

Some of the early makers produced side bead planes with double irons. The double iron principle was applied almost universally to bench planes but was apparently unsuccessful or unnecessary in moulding planes. Mouldings were always made from select straight grained stock which lessened the need for a top iron. Perhaps another reason for their lack of popularity was the difficulty in adjustment of the irons. The two irons were not connected together and the top one tended to move when the wedge was tightened.

Examination of several double iron bead planes reveal that the makers failed to allow enough throat for the shavings. All of the examples noted have been reworked to open the throats as can be seen in the illustrations. The top iron obviously curled the shavings enough to cause jamming in the standard sized moulding plane throat.

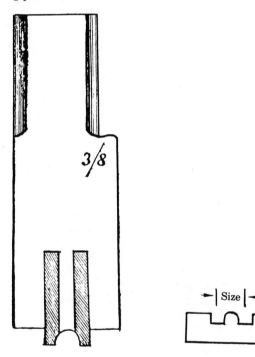

1857 (Ref. 13)

No. 6E1 Center Bead

6E1 CENTER BEAD

Also listed as a Single Bead Reeding Plane and as a One Bead Reeding Plane. Center was sometimes spelled Centre.

This type of moulding plane was used to cut a single decorative bead into a flat surface. It was widely used for ceiling boards.

Size: The size in inches is normally stamped on the heel. The following 12 sizes were offered: ⅛, 3/16, ¼, 5/16, ⅜, 7/16, ½, 9/16, ⅝, ¾, ⅞, 1 inches.

The size refers to the distance between centers of the grooves as shown in the illustration.

145

The critical wear points were generally made of boxwood to increase the life of the tool. They were either double boxed or solid boxed as shown in the boxwood insert sketch. The solid boxed variety has been noted only in smaller sizes. The boxwood insert was dovetailed into the plane in some cases.

double boxed   solid boxed

Boxwood Inserts

Center bead planes are often noted with holes drilled through the body such that the plane could be mounted on a pair of panel plow arms. Using a center bead with plow arms was a convenient method of beading a fixed distance from an edge without the necessity of fastening a fence to the workpiece. Plow arms could be bought separately from several planemakers if a special pair was desired for use with a center bead plane.

Sellens Collection

No. 6E2 Cock Bead

6E2   COCK BEAD
A cock bead is generally defined as a bead which extends above the surface surrounding it. The cock bead moulding plane cuts away the surface on both sides of the bead leaving the bead extended. Additional stock adjacent to the cut can then be easily removed with a bench plane.
Size: 3/16, ¼, ⅜, ½ inches. Size refers to the bead diameter.
The illustrated plane was made by Bodman & Hussey of Pawtucket, R.I.

No. 6E3 Cock Bead, Double Iron

6E3   COCK BEAD, DOUBLE IRON
Size: ¼ inch
The two irons of this plane are both ground to cut an identical bead. It is
probable that only one iron at a time was used depending upon the grain and
hardness of the wood being worked. The irons are bedded at different angles.
The plane was made by Montgomery of Boston, Mass.

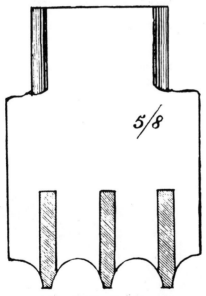

1857 (Ref. 13)

No. 6F1 Reeding Plane

6F1   REEDING PLANE
A plane that cuts two center beads was generally listed as a reeding plane.
Size: Size in inches is normally stamped on the heel. The following ten sizes
         were offered: ⅛, 3/16, ¼, 5/16, ⅜, ½, ⅝, ¾, ⅞, 1 inches
The size refers to the distance between centers of two adjacent grooves as
shown in the No. 6E1 center bead illustration.

147

No. 6F2 Reeding Plane - 3, 4, or 5 Bead

6F2   REEDING PLANE - 3, 4 or 5 Bead
Reeding planes were made that would work 3, 4 or 5 beads with one pass.
When the plane was more than two beads wide, the term reeding was always
followed by the number of beads. The plane was sometimes listed simply as a
3 bead, 4 bead or 5 bead.
Size: Size in inches is normally stamped on the heel. The following four
      sizes were offered: 3/16, ¼, ⅜, ½ inches.
The size refers to the distance between centers of two adjacent grooves as
shown in the No. 6E1 Center Bead illustration.

The plane shown in the illustration is a ¼ inch No. 152 made by Sandusky
Tool Company.

No. 6F3 Reeding Plane, Handled

6F3   REEDING PLANE, HANDLED
Length: 14 inches
Size: ⅞ inch bead
Most of the moulding plane types were available with handles but handled examples are not common. Note that the iron in the illustrated plane cuts only one bead. The adjacent bead is used as a guide or fence to properly position the bead being cut. This guide feature was sometimes listed as a follower and the plane would then be called a Bead with Follower.

Sellens Collection

No. 6F4 Bead Cluster

6F4   BEAD CLUSTER
This moulding tool will cut a cluster of three partial beads. Neither the name nor an illustration has been noted in available tool catalogs. The illustrated plane was made by M. Copeland.

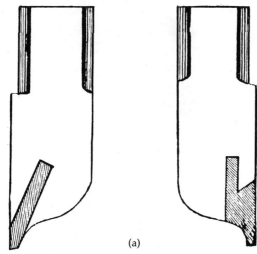

Single Box

Shoulder Box

(a)

1857 (Ref. 13)

No. 6G1 Snipe Bill

149

(b)

George Tuttle Collection

No. 6G1 Snipe Bill

6G1   SNIPE BILL
The snipe bills were always sold in pairs consisting of one each right hand and left hand planes. They did not cut a moulding by themselves but were used to clean out or deepen cuts made by other moulding planes.

Boxwood inserts were used to decrease wear on the narrow point. The two types of boxwood strips are shown in illustration (a). The shoulder boxed type were listed by some suppliers as full boxed, shoulder tipped or double boxed.

Sellens Collection

No. 6H1 Fluting Plane

6H1   FLUTING PLANE
Review of all available catalogs has failed to reveal a single listing of wooden fluting planes. However, planes that will make a semi-circular cut are fairly common and are known as fluting planes by craftsmen and collectors alike. A flute is normally considered to be a long vertical channel in a column or pilaster. Such a channel is usually semi-circular in cross section and several such channels are used parallel to each other.

150

The illustrated one inch flute plane has a fixed stop on both sides of the iron and screw holes on one side where a fence has been attached. It was made by G. & W.H. Roseboom of Cincinnati, Ohio.

This particular plane would also fully comply with the description of a small pump plane as listed by one supplier.

Complex Moulding Planes

Numerical listing of complex moulding planes.

Ref. No.	Name
7A1	Ogee
7A2	Ogee with Bevel
7A3	Ogee with Bead
7A4	Ogee with Astragal
7A5	Ogee with Square
7A6	Ogee with Bevel, 2 Irons
7A7	Ogee with Bevel, 2 Irons, Handled
7B1	Grecian Ogee
7B2	Grecian Ogee with Bevel
7B3	Grecian Ogee with Bead
7B4	Grecian Ogee with Fillet
7B5	Grecian Ogee with Astragal
7B6	Grecian Ogee with Quirk & Bead
7B7	Grecian Ogee with Bevel, Handled
7B8	Grecian Ogee with Fillet, Handled
7B9	Grecian Ogee with Bevel, 2 Irons
7C1	Roman Ogee
7D1	Quirk Ogee
7D2	Quirk Ogee with Bevel
7D3	Quirk Ogee with Bead
7D4	Quirk Ogee with Astragal
7D5	Quirk Ogee with Fillet
7E1	Reverse Ogee
7E2	Reverse Ogee, Flat
7E3	Reverse Ogee with Bead
7E4	Reverse Ogee with Astragal
7E5	Reverse Ogee with Astragal, Handled
7E6	Reverse Ogee with Square
7E7	Reverse Ogee with Square, Flat
7E8	Reverse Ogee with Two Squares
7E9	Reverse Ogee with Fence
7E10	Pilaster
7E11	Reverse Ogee, Flat, Handled
7E12	Cabinet Ogee
7F1	Roman Reverse Ogee
7F2	Roman Reverse Ogee with Fence
7G1	Grecian Ovolo
7G2	Grecian Ovolo with Bevel
7G3	Grecian Ovolo with Bead
7G4	Grecian Ovolo with Bead, Handled
7G5	Grecian Ovolo with Astragal
7G6	Grecian Ovolo with Square
7G7	Grecian Ovolo with Fillet
7H1	Quirk Ovolo
7H2	Quirk Ovolo with Bead
7J1	Gothic Bead
7K1	Cove with Bead

7L1	Door Moulding
7M1	P.G. Moulding
7N1	Nosing Moulding
7N2	Belection
7P1	Cornice Plane
7P2	Cornice Planes, Ogee
7P3	Cornice Plane, 2 Irons
7R1	Cove and Ogee Set

The planes that cut compound curves are grouped under the general heading of Complex Moulding Planes. The ogee alone and in combination with other shapes make up the largest single moulding type both in the number of varieties and in the number of planes extant.

As previously stated, an ogee is an S shaped symmetrical curve.

When a concave curve is joined to a convex curve of the same size and shape, a pleasing ogee contour much like an ocean wave and trough is formed.

A standard ogee moulding is constructed with the convex portion of the curve adjacent to the thickest part of the stock. Some reference books attempt to define the curve in terms of upper and lower portions but only create the additional question of which side of the moulding is up. Inasmuch as the ogee moulding is frequently used as a base, as well as for a cornice, it cannot be defined by reference to which portion is up.

The reverse ogee, or cyma reversa as it is called in the dictionaries, is simply the reverse of the standard ogee. The reverse ogee was also called a Back Ogee by some planemakers.

The Grecian ovolo was also a popular moulding shape alone and in combination. The ovolo, as used in this group, is the unsymmetrical curve rather than the quarter round called an ovolo by some makers. Quarter round shapes are listed under the heading of simple moulding planes.

Boxwood wear strips were used in many of the complex mouldings, particularly the Grecian varieties, to reduce wear at critical points and thereby increase the life of the tool. An occasional plane is seen with more than one boxwood insert.

Unless otherwise noted under the individual descriptions, each of the complex moulding planes is the standard length of approximately 9½ inches. The size in inches is normally stamped on the heel of the plane. Where a single number is used, it generally refers to the thickness of stock to be worked. Where two numbers are stamped on the heel, the second number normally defines the width of the moulding.

Most of the planes shown in this group were available with handles from one or more makers. Some makers listed handled planes separately in only the larger sizes but at least one supplier offered any size with a handle for fifty cents extra.

Some makers of wooden planes added to the terminology problem by listing some of the moulding planes under two headings. For instance, one supplier offered wide Ogee and Bevel planes and also offered the same tools on a different page and called them Base Planes. A base can be defined as the bottom moulding on a column, wall or pilaster. The base moulding was usually wide and fairly shallow and could be made up of almost any moulding contour. A wide ogee and bevel would make an excellent base moulding but should not be called a base plane in a definitive sense. The terms Band Moulding, Base and Band, Bed Moulding, Sur Base and Architrave are other names similarly applied to various moulding planes of different shapes. These terms applied to a possible or recommended usage of the tool and were not intended to be descriptive of the moulding shape.

A rear view of the planes are used here-in to show the contour of the plane soles and of the mouldings they produce.

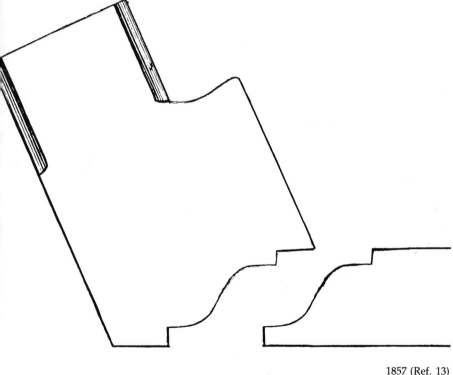

1857 (Ref. 13)

No. 7A1 Ogee

7A1   OGEE
       Sometimes listed as Plain Ogee or as a Common Ogee
       Sizes: Fourteen sizes to cut the following moulding widths were offered: ³/₈, 7/16, ¹/₂, ⁵/₈, ³/₄, ⁷/₈, 1, 1¹/₈, 1¹/₄, 1³/₈, 1¹/₂, 1³/₄, 2, 2¹/₄ inches.

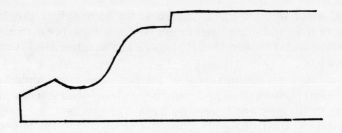

No. 7A2 Ogee with Bevel

7A2   OGEE WITH BEVEL
       Sizes: Fourteen sizes to cut the following moulding widths were offered: 3/8,
       1/2, 5/8, 3/4, 7/8, 1, 1 1/8, 1 1/4, 1 3/8, 1 1/2, 1 5/8, 1 3/4, 1 7/8, 2 inches.

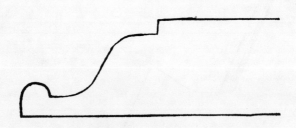

No. 7A3 Ogee with Bead

7A3   OGEE WITH BEAD
       Sizes: Eleven sizes to cut the following moulding widths were offered: 3/8,
       1/2, 5/8, 3/4, 7/8, 1, 1 1/4, 1 3/8, 1 1/2, 1 3/4, 2 inches.

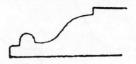

1889 (Ref. 34)

No. 7A4 Ogee with Astragal

7A4   OGEE WITH ASTRAGAL
       Also listed as an Ogee with Torus Bead.
       Sizes: Twelve sizes to cut the following moulding widths were offered: 3/8,
       1/2, 5/8, 3/4, 7/8, 1, 1 1/8, 1 1/4, 1 3/8, 1 1/2, 1 3/4, 2 inches.

156

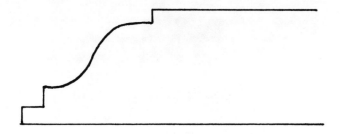

No. 7A5 Ogee with Square

7A5 OGEE WITH SQUARE
Sizes: Ten sizes to cut the following moulding widths were offered: ⅜, ½, ⅝, ¾, ⅞, 1, 1¼, 1½, 1¾, 2 inches.

No. 7A6 Ogee with Bevel, 2 Irons

7A6 OGEE WITH BEVEL, 2 IRONS
The illustrated plane is marked W.W. Williams. The size marked on the heel is 9/8 x 2. This variety of plane was not included in any available supplier catalog or price list.

No. 7A7 Ogee with Bevel, 2 Irons, Handled

7A7   OGEE WITH BEVEL, 2 IRONS, HANDLED
The illustrated plane is marked S.S. Barry N. York. It is 14 inches long and has a 3 inch iron. The second iron cuts the bevel only. This variety of plane has not been noted in any supplier catalog or listing.

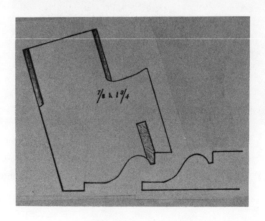

1857 (Ref. 13)

No. 7B1 Grecian Ogee

7B1   GRECIAN OGEE
Sizes: Thirteen sizes to cut the following moulding widths were offered: 3/8, 7/16, 1/2, 5/8, 3/4, 7/8, 1, 1 1/8, 1 1/4, 1 1/2, 1 3/4, 2, 2 1/4 inches.

158

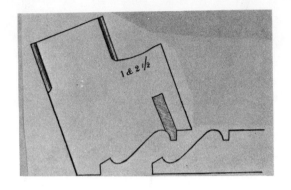

1857 (Ref. 13)

No. 7B2 Grecian Ogee with Bevel

7B2   GRECIAN OGEE WITH BEVEL
The larger sizes were also listed as Base Planes.
Sizes: Sixteen sizes to cut the following moulding widths were offered: ⅜,
½, 7/16, ⅝, ¾, ⅞, 1, 1⅛, 1¼, 1½, 1¾, 2, 2¼, 2½, 2¾, 3 inches.

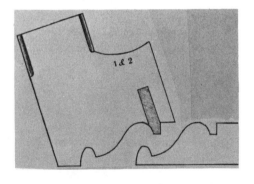

1857 (Ref. 13)

No. 7B3 Grecian Ogee with Bead

7B3   GRECIAN OGEE WITH BEAD
Sizes: Thirteen sizes to cut the following moulding widths were offered: ⅜,
½, ⅝, ¾, ⅞, 1, 1⅛, 1¼, 1½, 1¾, 2, 2¼, 2½ inches.

159

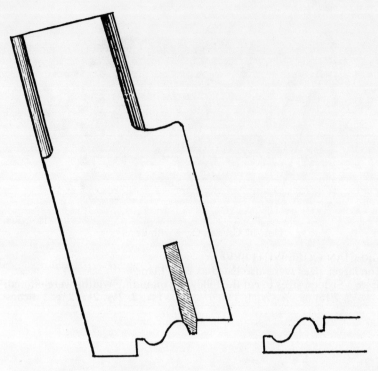

1857 (Ref. 13)

No. 7B4 Grecian Ogee with Fillet

7B4 GRECIAN OGEE WITH FILLET
Also listed as a Grecian Ogee with Square.
Sizes: Ten sizes to cut the following moulding widths were offered: 3/8, 1/2, 5/8, 3/4, 7/8, 1, 1 1/4, 1 1/2, 1 3/4, 2 inches.

1889 (Ref. 34)

No. 7B5 Grecian Ogee with Astragal

7B5 GRECIAN OGEE WITH ASTRAGAL
Also listed as Grecian Ogee with Torus Bead.
Sizes: Nine sizes to cut the following moulding widths were offered: 3/8, 1/2, 5/8, 3/4, 1, 1 1/4, 1 1/2, 1 3/4, 2 inches.

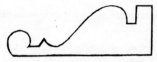

No. 7B6 Grecian Ogee with Quirk and Bead

7B6   GRECIAN OGEE WITH QUIRK AND BEAD
Also listed as a Band Ogee.
Sizes: Ten sizes to cut the following moulding widths were offered: ¾, 1,
1⅛, 1¼, 1⅜, 1½, 1⅝, 1¾, 1⅞, 2 inches.
This moulding shape was not a common pattern. It was listed as being made
to order by Ohio Tool Company and was not listed at all by most suppliers.

George Tuttle Collection

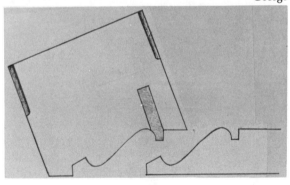

1857 (Ref. 13)

No. 7B7 Grecian Ogee with Bevel, Handled

7B7   GRECIAN OGEE WITH BEVEL, HANDLED
Also listed as a Base Plane
Sizes: Five sizes to cut the following moulding widths were offered: 2, 2¼,
2½, 2¾, 3 inches. Thickness of stock to be worked by the larger planes
was generally somewhat less than one half the width of the moulding.
An example of size is 1 x 2½ inches.
The illustrated plane is marked Gardner and Murdock, Boston. It was made
to work ⅞ inch stock and has a 3 inch iron. The sole is 14½ inches long.

No. 7B8 Grecian Ogee with Fillet, Handled

7B8   GRECIAN OGEE WITH FILLET, HANDLED
The illustrated plane is an example of the larger sized moulding planes with a razee tote. This particular one has a separate iron to cut the top of the fillet.

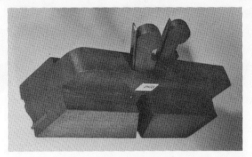

No. 7B9 Grecian Ogee with Bevel, 2 Irons

7B9   GRECIAN OGEE WITH BEVEL, 2 IRONS
The illustrated plane cuts a common moulding pattern but is unique in that it has a separate iron for cutting the bevel.

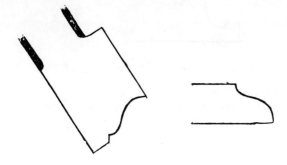

1880 (Ref. 15)

No. 7C1 Roman Ogee

7C1   ROMAN OGEE

This type of plane was listed by the Ohio Tool Company as a "Roman Ogee with Fence to work the edge of a board."

Sizes: Seven sizes to cut the following moulding widths were offered: 3/8, 1/2, 5/8, 3/4, 7/8, 1, 1 1/4 inches. The thickness of stock and width of the finished moulding are approximately equal.

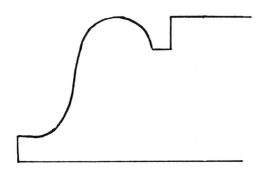

No. 7D1 Quirk Ogee

7D1   QUIRK OGEE

Sizes: Ten sizes to cut moulding widths as follows were offered: 3/8, 1/2, 5/8, 3/4, 7/8, 1, 1 1/4, 1 1/2, 1 3/4, 2 inches.

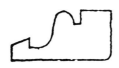

1889 (Ref. 34)

No. 7D2 Quirk Ogee with Bevel

7D2   QUIRK OGEE WITH BEVEL

Sizes: Nine sizes to cut the following moulding widths were offered: 3/8, 1/2, 5/8, 3/4, 1, 1 1/4, 1 1/2, 1 3/4, 2 inches.

No. 7D3 Quirk Ogee with Bead

7D3   QUIRK OGEE WITH BEAD
       Sizes: Nine sizes to cut the following moulding widths were offered: ⅜, ½, ⅝, ¾, ⅞, 1, 1¼, 1½, 2 inches.

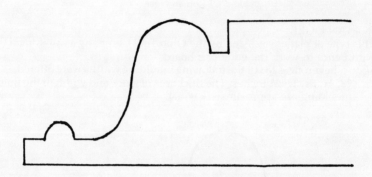

No. 7D4 Quirk Ogee with Astragal

7D4   QUIRK OGEE WITH ASTRAGAL
       Also listed as a Quirk Ogee with Bead and as a Qk Ogee with Astragal.
       Sizes: Ten sizes to cut the following moulding widths were offered: ⅜, ½, ⅝, ¾, ⅞, 1, 1¼, 1½, 1¾, 2 inches.

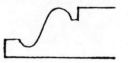

1889 (Ref. 34)

No. 7D5 Quirk Ogee with Fillet

7D5   QUIRK OGEE WITH FILLET
       Sizes: Nine sizes to cut the following moulding widths were offered: ⅜, ½, ⅝, ¾, 1, 1¼, 1½, 1¾, 2 inches.

164

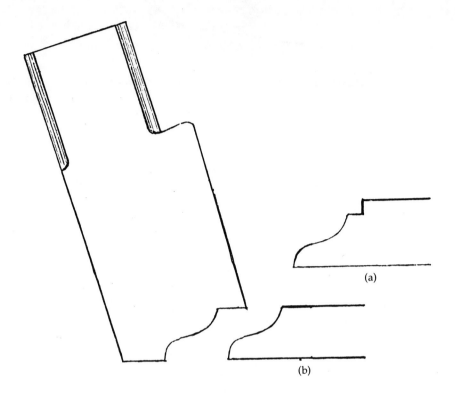

(a)

(b)

1872 (Ref. 18)

No. 7E1 Reverse Ogee

7E1   REVERSE OGEE
      Also known as a Lambs Tongue and as a Back Ogee
      Sizes: Thirteen sizes to cut the following moulding widths were offered: ¼,
        ⅜, ½, ⅝, ¾, ⅞, 1, 1¼, 1½, 1¾, 2, 2¼, 2½ inches.
      One supplier referred to the illustration (a) moulding shape as a feather edge
      ogee.

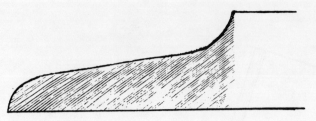

1857 (Ref. 13)

No. 7E2 Reverse Ogee, Flat

7E2   REVERSE OGEE, FLAT
       Also listed as a Grecian Reverse Ogee.
       Sizes: Fifteen sizes to cut the following moulding widths were offered. ⅜,
       ½, ⅝, ¾, ⅞, 1, 1⅛, 1¼, 1½, 1¾, 2, 2⅛, 2¼, 3 inches. Width of the
       moulding is 2 to 3 times the thickness of the stock.

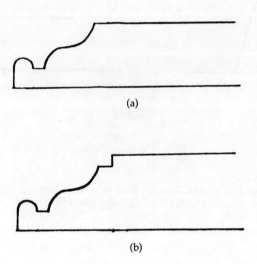

(a)

(b)

No. 7E3 Reverse Ogee with Bead

7E3   REVERSE OGEE WITH BEAD
       Also listed as a Back Ogee with Bead
       Sizes: Ten sizes to cut the following moulding widths were offered: ⅜, ½,
       ⅝, ¾, ⅞, 1, 1¼, 1½, 1¾, 2 inches.

166

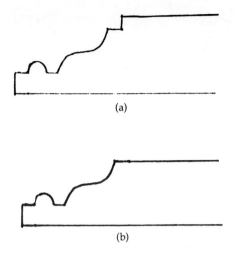

(a)

(b)

No. 7E4 Reverse Ogee with Astragal

7E4   REVERSE OGEE WITH ASTRAGAL
       Sizes: Six sizes to cut the following moulding widths were offered: ¾, 1, 1¼,
       1½, 1¾, 2 inches.

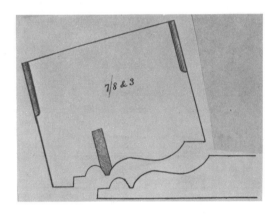

1857 (Ref. 13)

No. 7E5 Reverse Ogee with Astragal, Handled

7E5   REVERSE OGEE WITH ASTRAGAL, HANDLED
       This item was also listed as a Base Plane and as a Reverse Ogee with Bead.

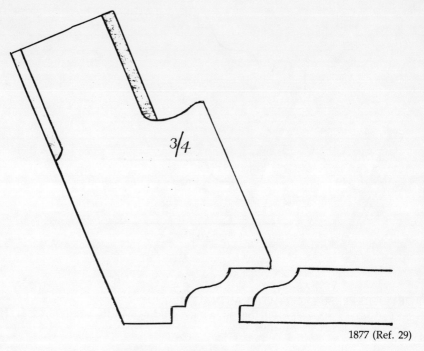

1877 (Ref. 29)

No. 7E6 Reverse Ogee With Square

7E6   REVERSE OGEE WITH SQUARE
Also listed as a Back Ogee with Square and Back Ogee with Fillet.
Sizes: Eleven sizes to cut moulding widths as follows were offered: ⅜, ½, ⅝, ¾, ⅞, 1, 1⅛, 1¼, 1½, 1¾, 2 inches. This plane is listed as a new style moulding in the 1877 Sandusky Tool Company Catalog.

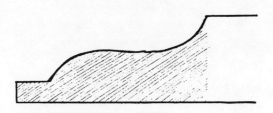

1872 (Ref. 18)

No. 7E7 Reverse Ogee with Square, Flat

7E7   REVERSE OGEE WITH SQUARE, FLAT
Also listed as a Reverse Ogee with Fillet.
Sizes: Fourteen sizes to cut moulding widths as follows were offered: ⅜, ½, ⅝, ¾, ⅞, 1, 1⅛, 1¼, 1½, 1¾, 2, 2¼, 2½, 3 inches. Planes of this type were often handled when made to cut mouldings of two inches or more.

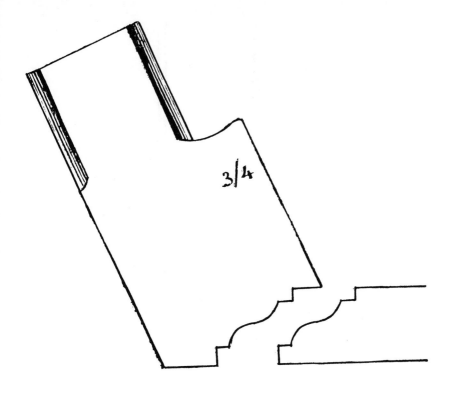

3/4

1857 (Ref. 13)

No. 7E8 Reverse Ogee with Two Squares

7E8   REVERSE OGEE WITH TWO SQUARES
Also listed as a Back Ogee with Double Fillet.
This pattern was listed by one supplier as a Reverse or Back Ogee with Square.
Sizes: Ten sizes were offered to cut moulding widths as follows: $3/8$, $1/2$, $5/8$, $3/4$, $7/8$, 1, $1\frac{1}{4}$, $1\frac{1}{2}$, $1\frac{3}{4}$, 2 inches.

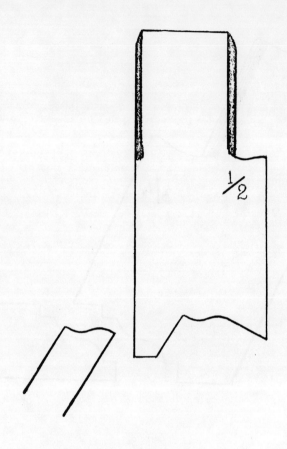

1877 (Ref. 20)

No. 7E9 Reverse Ogee with Fence

7E9   REVERSE OGEE WITH FENCE
    Sizes: Ten sizes were offered to cut moulding widths as follows: ⅜, ½, ⅝, ¾, ⅞, 1, 1¼, 1½, 1¾, 2 inches.

 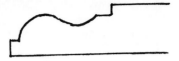

No. 7E10 Pilaster

7E10   PILASTER
        Width: 3½, 4 inches
        Several suppliers listed a pilaster moulding plane but the only noted illustra-
        tion of the type is included in Philip Chapin's broadside reprinted in Refer-
        ence 37.

        The architectural definition of a pilaster is an upright support such as that
        sometimes used on either side of an entrance or doorway. Pilasters are
        frequently fluted but are sometimes plain or plain with chamfered corners.
        This plane was probably intended to make the base or cap moulding of a
        particular type of pilaster.

George Tuttle Collection

No. 7E11 Reverse Ogee, Flat, Handled

7E11   REVERSE OGEE, FLAT, HANDLED
        Size: 3 inches
        This is an excellent example of a handled moulding plane. Some suppliers
        listed all moulding planes as being available with handles at extra cost.
        However, they are seldom seen except in the larger sizes and even those are
        quite scarce. The illustrated plane is marked No. 62 and was probably made
        by Ohio Tool Company.

171

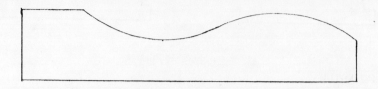

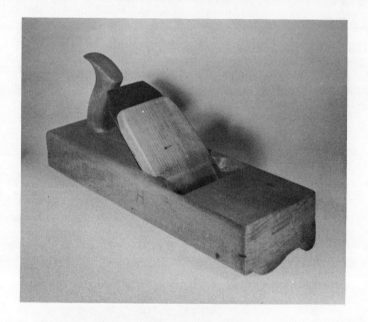

No. 7E12 Cabinet Ogee

7E12   CABINET OGEE
Also listed as a Cabinet Maker's Ogee or Cornice Ogee
Length: 14 inches approximately
Size: Ten sizes were offered as follows: 2, 2¼, 2½, 2¾, 3, 3¼, 3½, 4, 4½, 5
inches. Size refers to the width of the cut.
The illustrated plane is a 3 inch cabinet ogee sold by Shapleigh Day and Co. of
St. Louis. It is 14½ inches long. Some suppliers listed cabinet and cornice
ogees separately; however the difference, if any, has not been defined.

This type of plane is commonly labeled by tool collectors as a crown moulding
or cornice plane. It is probable that many mouldings made with the larger
sizes of these tools were used as cornices; however, the planemakers generally listed them as cabinet ogees.

172

Sellens Collection

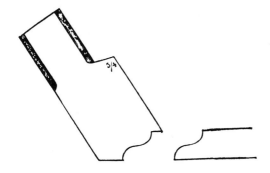

1880 (Ref. 15)

No. 7F1 Roman Reverse Ogee

7F1   ROMAN REVERSE OGEE
Sizes: Nine sizes were offered to cut moulding widths as follows: ³⁄₈, ½, ⁵⁄₈, ¾, ⁷⁄₈, 1, 1¼, 1½, 1¾ inches.
The plane shown in the illustration is stamped 1½ two places on the heel. It will cut a moulding 1½ inches wide on 1½ inch stock. It is a No. 62½ made by Ohio Tool Company.

173

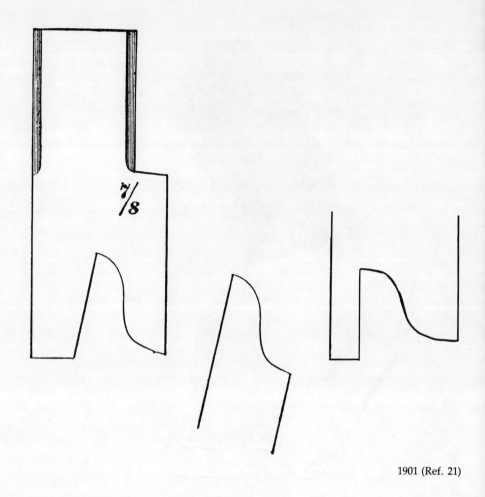

7/8

1901 (Ref. 21)

1880 (Ref. 15)

No. 7F2 Roman Reverse Ogee with Fence

7F2   ROMAN REVERSE OGEE WITH FENCE
       Sizes: Ten sizes were offered to cut moulding widths as follows: ⅜, ½, ⅝,
              ¾, ⅞, 1, 1¼, 1½, 1¾, 2 inches.
       Reference 6 (1897) stated that this was a new type of plane that was easier to
       work than previous types. It also stated that the plane was made to work on a
       slight spring and that the iron is skewed.

       Width of the moulding cut was the same or less than the thickness of stock to
       be worked.

174

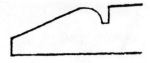

1889 (Ref. 34)

7G1 Grecian Ovolo

7G1   GRECIAN OVOLO
Ovolo was spelled Ovelo and Ovilo in some of the older listings.
Sizes: Thirteen sizes to cut the following moulding widths were offered: ⅜,
   ½, ⅝, ¾, ⅞, 1, 1⅛, 1¼, 1½, 1¾, 2, 2¼, 2½ inches.

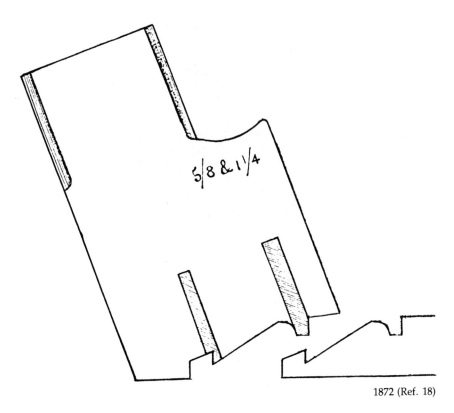

1872 (Ref. 18)

No. 7G2 Grecian Ovolo with Bevel

7G2   GRECIAN OVOLO WITH BEVEL
This plane is another example of the occasional disagreement on names. One
company referred to this type of plane as a Grecian Ovolo and Fillet. When
compared to the more common Grecian ogee shapes, there is little doubt that
it should have been listed as a bevel.
Sizes: Thirteen sizes to cut the following moulding widths were offered: ⅜,
   ½, ⅝, ¾, ⅞, 1, 1⅛, 1¼, 1½, 1¾, 2, 2¼, 2½ inches.

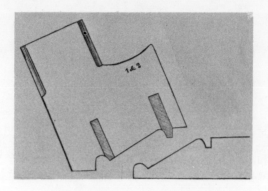

1857 (Ref. 13)

No. 7G3 Grecian Ovolo with Bead

7G3   GRECIAN OVOLO WITH BEAD
      Sizes: Thirteen sizes to cut the following moulding widths were offered: ⅜,
      ½, ⅝, ¾, ⅞, 1, 1⅛, 1¼, 1½, 1¾, 2, 2¼, 2½ inches.

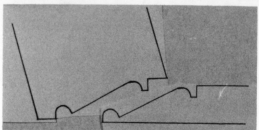

Sellens Collection

No. 7G4 Grecian Ovolo with Bead, Handled

7G4   GRECIAN OVOLO WITH BEAD, HANDLED
      Length: 14 inches.
      Sizes: Five sizes to cut the following moulding widths were offered: 2, 2¼,
      2½, 2¾, 3 inches.

176

The illustrated plane is 2½ inches wide and is made to work 1 inch stock. The center throat for easier discharge of shavings was a feature offered by some suppliers in the larger moulding planes. It was called a bench mouth by one supplier.

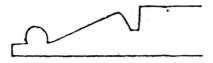

1889 (Ref. 34)

No. 7G5 Grecian Ovolo with Astragal

7G5 GRECIAN OVOLO WITH ASTRAGAL
Also listed as a Grecian Ovolo with Torus Bead
Sizes: Ten sizes to cut the following moulding widths were offered: ⅜, ½, ⅝, ¾, ⅞, 1¼, 1½, 1¾, 2 inches.

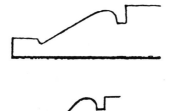

1889 (Ref. 34)

1901 (Ref. 1)

No. 7G6 Grecian Ovolo with Square

7G6 GRECIAN OVOLO WITH SQUARE
Also listed as a Grecian Ovolo with Raised Square
Sizes: Thirteen sizes to cut the following moulding widths were offered: ⅜, ½, ⅝, ¾, ⅞, 1, 1⅛, 1¼, 1½, 1¾, 2, 2¼, 2½ inches.

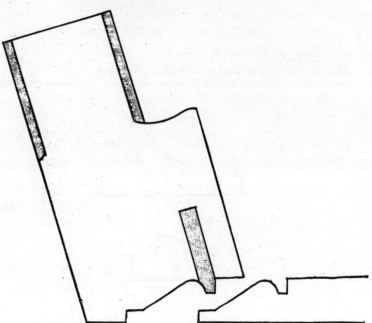

No. 7G7 Grecian Ovolo with Fillet

7G7 GRECIAN OVOLO WITH FILLET
Sizes: Thirteen sizes were offered to cut moulding widths as follows: ⅜, ½, ⅝, ¾, ⅞, 1, 1⅛, 1¼, 1½, 1¾, 2, 2¼, 2½ inches.
The plane shown in the illustration was made by Reed of Utica. It will work a moulding 1¾ inches wide on 1 inch stock. It is marked 8/8 on the heel.

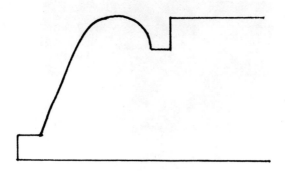

No. 7H1 Quirk Ovolo

7H1   QUIRK OVOLO
   Sizes: Ten sizes to cut moulding widths as follows were offered: ⅜, ½, ⅝,
   ¾, ⅞, 1, 1¼, 1½, 1¾, 2 inches.

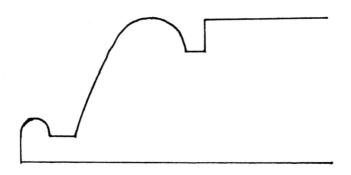

No. 7H2 Quirk Ovolo with Bead

7H2   QUIRK OVOLO WITH BEAD
   Sizes: Ten sizes to cut moulding widths as follows were offered: ⅜, ½, ⅝,
   ¾, ⅞, 1, 1¼, 1½, 1¾, 2 inches.

Sellens Collection

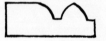

1901 (Ref. 1)

No. 7J1 Gothic Bead

7J1   GOTHIC BEAD
   Sizes: Nine sizes were offered to cut moulding widths as follows: ¼, ⅜, ½, ⅝, ¾, ⅞, 1, 1¼, 1½ inches. Width of the moulding was slightly more than the thickness. An example of size is ⅝ x ¾ inches.

   These planes were available plain or boxed.

   The plane shown in the illustration is a ½ inch gothic bead made by E. F. Seybold of Cincinnati, Ohio. This plane cuts a square shouldered bead rather than the rounded type shown in the catalog illustration.

Sellens Collection

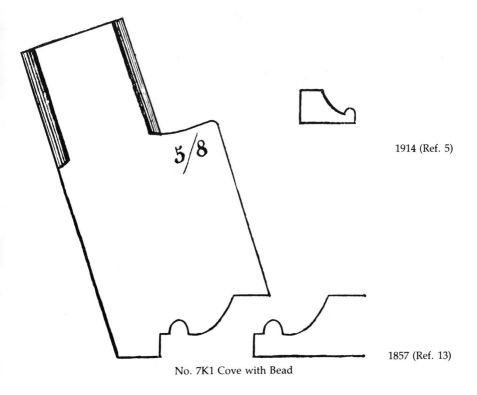

5/8

1914 (Ref. 5)

1857 (Ref. 13)

No. 7K1 Cove with Bead

7K1   COVE WITH BEAD
      This plane was also listed as a Scotia with Bead.
      Sizes: Eight sizes were listed to cut moulding widths as follows: 3/8, 1/2, 5/8,
         3/4, 7/8, 1, 1 1/4, 1 1/2 inches.
      The plane shown in the illustration is a one inch cove with bead marked
      Collins Ravenna. Width of the cut is 1 1/8 inches and overall width of the plane
      is 2 1/8 inches.

1914 (Ref. 5)

No. 7L1 Door Moulding

7L1   DOOR MOULDING
   Sizes: Seven sizes were offered to cut moulding widths as follows: ½, ¾, 1, 1¼, 1½, 1¾, 2 inches.

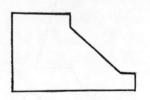

1914 (Ref. 5)

No. 7M1 P.G. Moulding

7M1   P.G. MOULDING
   Sizes: The following six sizes were offered: ½, ⅝, ¾, ⅞, 1, 1¼ inches.

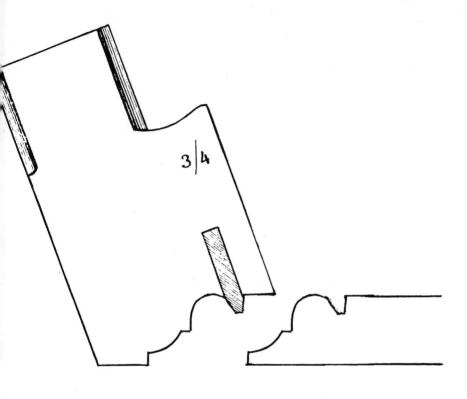

3|4

1857 (Ref. 13)

No. 7N1 Nosing Moulding

7N1 NOSING MOULDING

This type of plane was also listed as a Torus Bead and Cove, Belection, Bilection, Nosing Bilection and as a Belection with Quirk.

Sizes: Eleven sizes were offered to cut moulding widths as follows: ¼, ½, ⅝, ¾, ⅞, 1, 1⅛, 1¼, 1½, 1¾, 2 inches. Thickness of the stock is slightly more than one half the width of the moulding cut. An example of size is 1 x 1¾ inches.

The term Belection originally referred to a class of mouldings that would project beyond the surface of the item on which it is applied. For instance, if a belection was used around a door panel, it would project beyond the surface of the side stiles or frames. It does not appear that this nosing moulding could be readily used in that manner; however, the plane makers were explicit in their names and descriptions. Apparently the words belection, bilection, and bolection were merely variations in spelling of the same item.

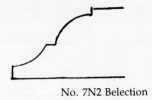

No. 7N2 Belection

7N2   BELECTION
        Also called a Bilection.
        These planes were made in sizes up to two inches. See item 7N1 for comments regarding belection mouldings. One use for this moulding was for application around a door panel or similar framed panel. The lower corner was rabbeted out so that the moulding would span the joint of the panel and the frame.

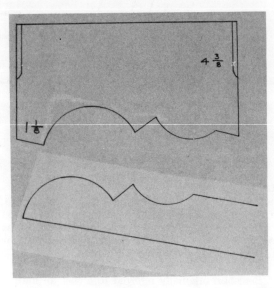

Carl Bopp Collection

(a)   No. 7P1 Cornice Plane

184

7P1   CORNICE PLANE
Length: 14 to 15 inches
The plane shown in illustration (a) was made by the Ohio Tool Company but does not have a series number as generally used by that maker. Perhaps it was a custom made item. It is 14⅞ inches long and has an open tote. Scribed spring lines and size markings on the heel leave little doubt as to the moulding it was meant to produce. Illustration (b) shows a plane that cuts a similar moulding. Note that it is constructed opposite of the other plane and uses a fixed fence. This plane is 14 inches long and is marked M. Adams.

Cornice planes are called crown moulding planes by many collectors and writers but were apparently never called that by the makers and sellers. The name evolved from the practice of using a wide moulding at the top or crown of a pillar, room or outside wall. The tool used to make this top moulding became known as a crown plane or crown moulding plane.

1872 (Ref. 18)

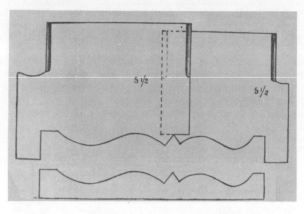

1857 (Ref. 13)

No. 7P2 Cornice Planes, Ogee

7P2   CORNICE PLANES, OGEE
These planes were sold in pairs as can be seen in the illustrations. Each plane cut a portion of the moulding contour.
Sizes: The following sizes were offered: 4, 4½, 5 and 5½ inches.
Size refers to the overall width of the finished moulding which was made by the cuts of two different planes on the same workpiece.

186

No. 7P3 Cornice Plane, 2 Irons

7P3   CORNICE PLANE, 2 IRONS
Length: 15¾ inches
Width: 4 inch cut
This unique cornice plane is fashioned with 2 irons staggered such that a center rib is left in the plane body. The plane is marked R. Barnes on the toe end.

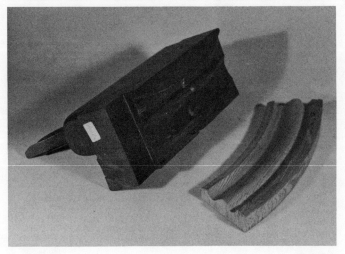

No. 7R1 Cove and Ogee Set

7R1   COVE AND OGEE SET

The moulding contour that can be cut by the illustrated planes might best be described as a cove and ogee design. This moulding shape is not unique but has not been positively correlated with a name used by the plane makers. The unique feature of this set is that one plane cuts a straight piece of moulding and the shorter plane is designed to continue the same moulding shape around a curve. The handled plane is 13½ inches long and the short one is 8 inches long.

Coopers' Planes

Numerical listing of coopers' planes.

Ref. No.	Name
8A1	Coopers' Jointer
8A2	Coopers' Jointer, Two Irons
8B1	Leveling Plane
8B2	Leveling Plane, Keg
8C1	Howel, Tight Barrel
8C2	Howel, Gouge
8C3	Howel, Beer
8C4	Howel, Shifting
8D1	Croze, Tight Barrel
8D2	Croze, V
8D3	Croze, Beer
8D4	Croze, Tank or Hogshead
8D5	Croze, Shifting
8D6	Croze, Beer Post
8D7	Croze, Salt Barrel
8D8	Croze, Seigfried's Patent
8D9	Croze, Atchison
8D10	Croze, Crane's Patent
8D11	Croze, Post
8D12	Croze, Shifting, Tight Barrel
8E1	Head Float
8E2	Head Float, Cleveland Pattern
8F1	Head Cutter
8G1	Rounding Plane
8H1	Combination Howel and Croze
8H2	Combination Leveling and Howel
8H3	Combination Leveling and Croze

A cooper is the craftsman who makes wooden barrels or other staved containers. Barrel making was a widespread craft that flourished prior to the twentieth century wherever goods was packaged for shipment. The barrel was known as the perfect container and was used for transport of most everything from whiskey to crockery. The coopered vessel was popular because it was strong both inside and out, was made from natural material and could be made with hand labor with a minimum of tools. The corrugated pasteboard box and the use of metal containers led to the downfall of the barrel and now it has little use except for the aging of whiskey. The making and repair of whiskey barrels is still a sizeable business but most of the work is now done by machinery.

Tools used by the cooper evolved over years of usage into a highly specialized set of equipment that was good for little else than the intended function. They were not only specialized to barrel making but some were further specialized to a branch of the craft. The branches of coopering are generally specified as that of the wet cooper who made containers that would hold liquid (tight barrels) and the dry cooper who made barrels for non-liquids (dry or slack barrels). The white cooper who made buckets, tubs and similar items and the makers of beer containers were further specialists within the general branch of wet coopering. The beer container had to be particularly strong to contain the gas pressure and was therefore generally made of thick material with the head set deep within each end. The thick head material required a wide groove for seating the head into the side staves. Oak was used for making whiskey barrels and was generally used for beer barrels. The dry cooper used most any kind of wood depending upon the intended use of his product. Containers for heavy material obviously required the use of stronger and thicker wood than was required for the making of apple barrels for example. Dry work did not require close tolerance fits between the joints and therefore required less skill than that required of the wet cooper.

The most impressive of the coopers planes was the jointer. This plane did not have a rear tote in that it always remained stationary while the workpiece was drawn over the sole. It was fastened to the top of a low workbench or fitted with legs to stand on the floor. For floor mounting, the toe would have two legs or a Y shaped leg inserted into holes in the plane body. The heel was often notched to accept a heel block or plate which raised the heel a few inches from the floor and added stability to the assembly. Inasmuch as the toe end was set 2 or 3 feet higher than the heel, the cut was always made with the workpiece being moved downward along the plane sole. New jointers were neither notched nor drilled for attachment of mounting provisions. Mounting was apparently left entirely to the user as mounting fixtures were not offered in the catalogs. Jointers were available from commercial makers in practically every length from 2 ft. 10 inches to more than 6 feet. Homemade jointers up to 7½ feet have been noted.

The purpose of the howel was to cut a shallow concave groove a short distance from each end of the assembled staves. This groove was also called a howel. The howel provided a smooth surface in which to cut a sharp groove for insertion of the head. The sharp groove was known as a croze or croze groove and was cut by a plane called a croze. Both the croze and the howel planes were shaped to fit the inside curvature of the container being worked. The wooden piece holding the iron was called the block and the piece that slid on top of the staves and served as a fence was called the board. Inasmuch as the board slid continually on the end grain of the staves, it was subject to rapid wear and was often inlaid with iron, brass or lignum vitae.

The leveling plane was used to square and even the ends of the assembled staves prior to use of the howel and croze. The bevel immediately below the ends of the staves was called the chime or chine and was cut with a chamfer knife or coopers adze. Available American catalogs did not list a plane for cutting the chime and it definitely was not cut with a howel as stated in some descriptive literature. Brombacher (Ref. 32) listed an all-metal chamfer howel which was probably used to cut the howel and chime at the same time.

American tools and techniques of the cooper stemmed from British sources as did most American technology of the period. However, it appears the names of coopers tools vary widely from the names of similar items used in England and Scotland. American terminology is used in this volume.

1880 (Ref. 22)

No. 8A1 Coopers Jointer

8A1 COOPERS JOINTER
Also listed as a Long Jointer, Coopers Long Jointer and a Coopers Short Jointer.
Length: Commercially made jointers were available in a wide range of sizes.
The following specific lengths have been noted in suppliers literature:

2 feet, 10 inches	4½ feet
3 feet	4 feet, 8 inches
3 feet, 3 inches	5 feet
3 feet, 4 inches	5 feet, 4 inches
3½ feet (Beer keg tool)	5½ feet
4 feet, 3 inches	6 feet
4 feet, 4 inches	6 feet, 5 inches

Irons: 2½ to 4 inches wide. Single or double irons were available in all sizes of planes.

One supplier listed replacement irons of 2⅜ to 4 inches wide.

Wood Type: Beech, apple or maple

Coopers jointers were often longer than the actual workpiece and were not made to maneuver in the conventional manner. They were mounted upside down and the workpiece was passed over the plane and iron. The coopers jointer does not have a tote but may have holes or notches for attachment of legs and/or mounting brackets.

Some catalogs listed a choice of jointers for either heading or staves while other lists show certain jointers priced per pair. The L. and I.J. White catalog (Ref. 41) states that "A pair of Coopers' Jointers consists of one single iron heading and one double iron stave jointer." However, the same catalog offers heading jointers with either single or double irons. An article in the June 1974 issue of *The Chronicle* (Ref. 24) concludes that the iron of a heading jointer is slightly convex while that of a stave jointer is concave. One supplier offered to dowel the heading and stave jointers together for fifty cents extra.

William P. Graves Collection

No. 8A2 Coopers Jointer, Two Irons

8A2   COOPERS JOINTER, TWO IRONS

Size: 5 feet, 5½ feet or 6 feet

Many coopers jointers have two irons side-by-side in a single stock. Greenfield Tool Company (Ref. 18) lists three sizes of this type plane with either single or double irons. They are listed as a jointer "for head and stave in one stock." Several examples of two iron jointers have been noted that will accept one single iron and one double iron. It is believed that these planes are not head and stave jointers but are intended merely to provide handy access to both a rough cut and a finish cut plane. The illustrated plane is a two iron jointer with one single and one double iron.

1914 (Ref. 5)

No. 8B1 Leveling Plane

192

8B1   LEVELING PLANE

Also called a Leveler or a Leveller. Many tool collectors refer to this tool as a Sun Plane, however a thorough review of all available American maker and dealer literature has failed to uncover any reference to that name. The Sun Plane terminology is apparently a unique British name that was not generally adopted by American makers. It is therefore concluded that this tool should be called a leveling plane at least when referring to American items.

Width of Iron: 2 to 2⅛ inches

Wood Type: Beech, apple, lignum vitae, birch or cherry

Length: Leveling planes were listed in most catalogs without reference to size. It is probable that these advertised planes were the proper curvature to work a standard barrel inasmuch as the barrel was the most common size of coopered containers. The catalogs catering directly to the coopers trade listed leveling planes in accordance with the size of the container to be worked. The following sizes were offered. 3 gallon, 5 gallon, 10 gallon, ½ barrel, barrel, tierce, hogshead, puncheon, pipe and tank.

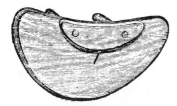

1885 (Ref. 31)

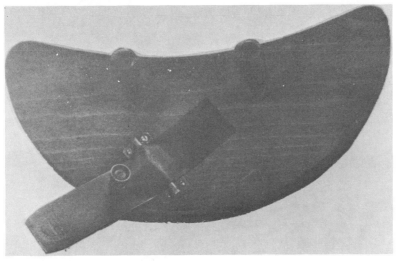

No. 8B2 Leveling Plane, Keg

8B2   LEVELING PLANE, KEG

Iron Width: 1½ inches

Wood: Apple

This tool was listed as a Hodgman's pattern for syrup and fish kegs. Leveling planes of this general type are usually of light construction and obviously made to work small or lightweight containers.

193

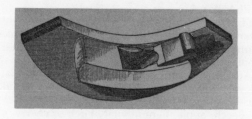

1880 (Ref. 22)

No. 8C1 Howel, Tight Barrel

8C1 HOWEL, TIGHT BARREL
Also listed as a Stock Howel
Sizes: Separate sizes were offered to work the following sizes of vessels: 3
gallon, 5 gallon, 10 gallon, ½ barrel, barrel, 18 inch salmon barrel, 20 inch
wine barrel, oil barrel, tierce or puncheon (24 to 40 inch) and hogshead.
Wood Type: Beech or apple
Iron Width: 2 to 3 inches
The top board was listed by some makers as being made of maple. One maker
offered lignum vitae inserts at extra cost.

1885 (Ref. 31)

No. 8C2 Howel, Gouge

8C2 HOWEL, GOUGE
Size: Four sizes to work the following containers were offered: 5 gallon, 10
gallon, ½ barrel and barrel.
Iron Width: 1⅛ to 1½ inches
Wood: Beech or apple
The gouge howel is essentially the same as a stock howel except that the iron
is slightly narrower. This type of howel was used primarily for dry barrel
work but one maker lists a gouge howel for oil barrels.

194

1922 (Ref. 32)

No. 8C3 Howel, Beer

8C3 HOWEL, BEER
Sizes: Eight sizes to work the following containers were offered: 5 gallon, 10 gallon, ⅛ barrel, 1/6 barrel, ¼ barrel, ½ barrel, barrel, hogshead.
Iron Width: 2½ to 3 inches
Wood Type: Beech or apple. Some were listed with a maple top board.
A beer howel is essentially the same as a tight barrel howel except that the beer howel has a wider iron that is positioned further from the top board. This results in the barrel head being positioned deeper into the barrel making a stronger container. Beer howels were made with and without the handle shown in the illustration.

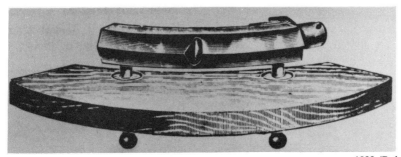

1922 (Ref. 32)

No. 8C4 Howel, Shifting

8C4 HOWEL, SHIFTING
This unique adjustable tool was listed as a New Jersey Shifting Howel with Brass Block. It was probably intended for use in repair work.

195

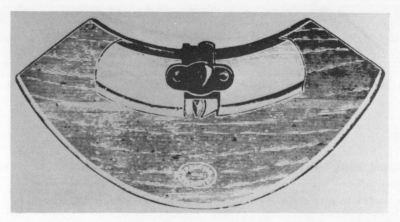

1922 (Ref. 32)

No. 8D1 Croze, Tight Barrel

8D1 CROZE, TIGHT BARREL
Also listed as a Lance Croze.
Sizes: The following sizes were offered: 3 gallon, 5 gallon, 10 gallon, ½ barrel, 18 inch salmon barrel, 20 inch wine barrel, tierce & puncheon (24 to 40 inch) and hogshead.
Wood Type: Beech, apple or lignum vitae. Some were listed with a maple top board and with lignum vitae inserts at the wear points of the top board.
The standard tight barrel croze had a 1/16 or 3/32 inch wide cutter. Wider cutters were available but a croze with an extra wide cutter was probably meant to be used on a beer barrel.

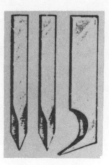

Lance Croze Irons

196

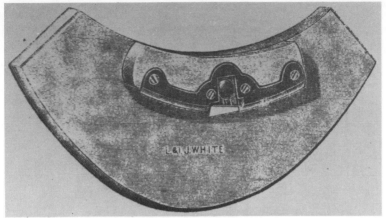

1912 (Ref. 41)

V Croze Iron

1922 (Ref. 32)

No. 8D2 Croze, V

8D2   CROZE, V

Three sizes were offered as follows: 14½ inch circle, 18 inch circle, barrel.

Wood Type: Beech, apple, lignum vitae, beech with an apple face, apple with a brass face, beech with a lignum vitae face or beech with a brass face. Maple boards were available from one supplier.

This type of croze was used for flour barrels and similar dry containers.

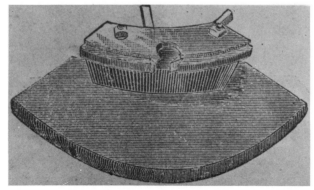

1906 (Ref. 30)

No. 8D3 Croze, Beer

197

8D3   CROZE, BEER
   Sizes: The following seven sizes were offered:
         5 gallon - ⅜ groove
         10 gallon - ½ inch groove
         ¼ barrel - ¼ inch groove
         1/6 barrel
         ¼ barrel - ¼ inch groove
         ½ barrel - ⅝ inch groove
         barrel - 11/16 inch groove
   Wood Type: Beech or apple

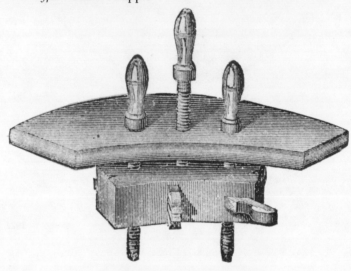

No. 8D4 Croze, Tank or Hogshead

8D4   CROZE, TANK OR HOGSHEAD
   Also called a Beer Hogshead Croze
   Size: Adjustable. Will cut a groove ¾, 1, 1¼, 1½, or 1¾ inches wide.
   Wood Type: Beech
   This type of adjustable croze is intended to be used on large beer containers.

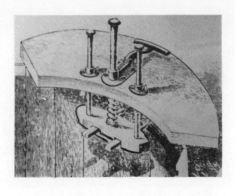

1922 (Ref. 32)

No. 8D5 Croze, Shifting

8D5   CROZE, SHIFTING
       Listed as a New Jersey Shifting Croze. This tool was probably intended for
       use in repair work.

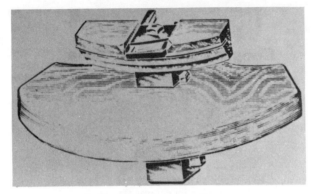

1922 (Ref. 32)

No. 8D6 Croze, Beer Post

8D6   CROZE, BEER POST
       Size: Five sizes were offered for use on the following containers: ⅛ barrel, ¼
              barrel, ½ barrel, barrel and hogshead.
       Iron Width: ⅜ to 1 inch

1922 (Ref. 32)

No. 8D7 Croze, Salt Barrel

8D7   CROZE, SALT BARREL
       Also called an Iron Block croze.
       Size: Listed in two sizes to work barrels and half barrels.
       The block was made of iron.

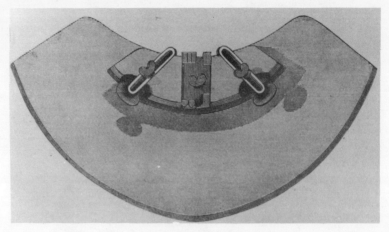

1877 (Ref. 29)

No. 8D8 Croze, Seigfried's Patent

8D8   CROZE, SEIGFRIED'S PATENT
       This croze was adjustable to work any size circle.
       Wood Type: Beech with a beech, maple or apple fence.

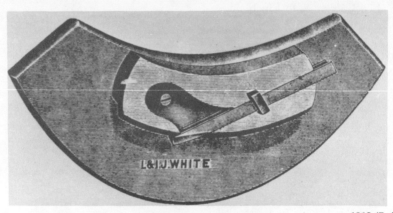

1912 (Ref. 41)

No. 8D9 Croze, Atchison

8D9   CROZE, ATCHISON
       Wood Type: Apple, apple with lignum vitae block, maple with lignum vitae
           block or lignum vitae.
       The Atchison croze was intended for use on flour barrels and other dry
       containers.

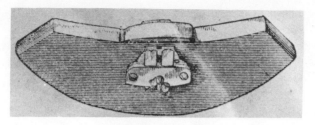

1906 (Ref. 30)

No. 8D10 Croze, Crane's Patent

8D10   CROZE, CRANE'S PATENT
For all sizes of casks and for all tight work. This croze was adjustable to cut the groove any distance below the chime.

1912 (Ref. 41)

No. 8D11 Croze, Post

8D11   CROZE, POST
This is a lance croze with the block attached to a post such that it can be adjusted for depth. It was intended for repair of beer containers of various sizes.

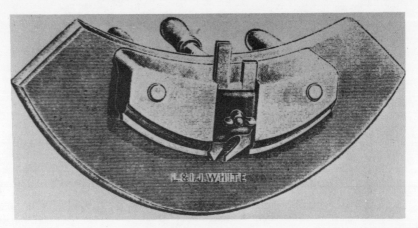

1912 (Ref. 41)

No. 8D12 Croze, Shifting, Tight Barrel

8D12　CROZE, SHIFTING, TIGHT BARREL
This is another type of adjustable croze that was probably intended for repair work on various sizes of casks.
Wood Type:　Beech or apple

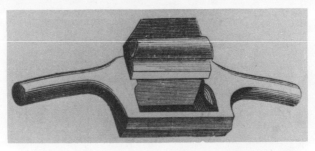

1877 (Ref. 29)

No. 8E1 Head Float

8E1　HEAD FLOAT
Also called a Heading Float or a Float Plane.
This tool was used to smooth the surface of the barrel head after the heading boards were doweled together.
Iron Width:　4 to 4½ inches
Wood Type:　Apple, lignum vitae, beech with an apple face, beech with a lignum vitae face.

202

No. 8E2 Head Float, Cleveland Pattern

8E2   HEAD FLOAT, CLEVELAND PATTERN
The Cleveland head float has an iron base faced with hardwood. The handles are wood. The illustrated plane is marked J.C. Steiger, Cleveland.

1906 (Ref. 30)

No. 8F1 Head Cutter

8F1   HEAD CUTTER
Adjustable to cut 12 to 21 inch diameter heads.
The catalog states "For cutting out heads to exact size, leaving a smooth, clean bevel to fit in the croze."

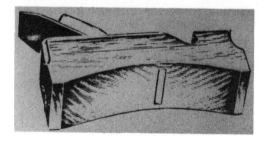

1922 (Ref. 32)

No. 8G1 Rounding Plane

8G1 ROUNDING PLANE
Actual size of this tool is not known. One supplier listed the plane as being suitable for all size work.

No. 8H1 Combination Howel and Croze

8H1 COMBINATION HOWEL AND CROZE
The illustrated plane was used for making apple barrels in the eastern Massachusetts area. The combination coopers tools were generally intended for dry cooper work or for small containers where a lightweight tool was satisfactory.

No. 8H2 Combination Leveling and Howel

8H2 COMBINATION LEVELING AND HOWEL
This is another lightweight combination tool used for making apple barrels.

No. 8H3 Combination Leveling and Croze

8H3 COMBINATION LEVELING AND CROZE

This scarce type of combination coopers tool and the two previous combination planes were all obtained in the same area of Massachusetts. They are unmarked but are obviously the product of a skilled tool maker and all appear similar in detail. It is probable that this maker specialized in tools for the local trade and never bothered to sign his work.

Homemade Wooden Planes

Wooden planes made by the user are seen in an infinite variety of shapes and sizes. Assuming that most of these planes extant in America were made after plane-making became a specialized craft, we can only speculate as to why an individual user may have made his own planes rather than buying commercial items. The availability of commercial tools could well have been a problem in remote areas or small villages and cost was a possible consideration. A skilled craftsman might choose to make his own tools during slack periods but could scarcely afford the time to make a plane that was needed immediately on the job. Most homemade planes are fitted with commercial irons which would indicate that commercial items were generally available. It is difficult to imagine a situation in which an iron but not the entire plane was available for sale. In some specialized cases, transportation problems prohibited the transfer of bulky and heavy items. In such cases, the craftsman may have carried along his plane irons and made the wooden plane bodies upon arrival at his remote destination.

Most of the homemade planes that are seen in shops and flea markets are essentially crude equivalents of commercial items. It might be argued that the standard commercial types actually are copies of the craftsman made tools and such was certainly true to some extent. Most of the standard items evolved from European tools made and used by the craftsmen before plane-making became a specialized craft.

An interesting facet of these one-of-a-kind planes is the variety of woods used in making them. Many were apparently made of whatever wood happened to be available at the moment. Beech was the most popular because this was the standard wood used for making small tools. Apple, maple, walnut, oak, birch and ash were widely available in America and were used for plane-making to some degree. Planes made of such unlikely material as hickory and pine has also been noted in a few cases. There are many unmarked rosewood and lignum vitae bench plane in shops and collections close to the port cities of the east coast. These planes are often narrow and razee shaped. It is generally accepted that they were used in the ship building trades. The reason for use of the rare woods for this particular type of planes is unknown except that these imported woods were more readily available in seaport towns than elsewhere.

Attempting to categorize homemade planes is an impossible task but some general grouping is attempted for purposes of discussion. The largest group consists merely of equivalents to commercial planes without apparent attempt to improve or to change the function. Many of these have a frill or decoration that makes them unique or desirable to some collectors but they are of little interest from a historical standpoint except in those rare cases where the plane is dated.

A second group of homemade planes are the miniatures or scaled down versions of the tools available commercially. It is generally assumed by collectors that these were made for use in doing precise work where a small tool was necessary. Instrument makers, pattern makers, etc. would certainly have a need for such tools but it is speculated that some and perhaps most of them were made without a definite use in mind. Making a miniature tool for a toy or a gift or merely as a rainy day pastime would be a normal project for a skilled woodworking craftsman. A special category of small planes with short soles and squirrel-tail handles are generally referred to as coachmakers planes. They may well have been used by coachmakers but the size and short soles make them equally well adapted for any intricate curved work. Planes of this type were made commercially in France but a thorough review of all available catalogs has failed to reveal a single listing by American makers. They were included in French catalogue listings of special tools for both coachmakers and stairbuilders.

Reworked commercial planes can be considered in the homemade category in that they were fashioned to accomplish a particular task. The hollow and round planes were often reworked to make a V or a bevel or some other special shape. The jack could be turned into a good gutter plane with minimum effort. The common smooth plane could be easily cut away to make a compass plane, hollowed out to make an oar plane or cut off to make a bullnose. There are rabbet planes that have been reworked to cut a moulding and moulding planes that have shaved off to cut a rabbet. Fortunately, most of these rework jobs are obvious but a few are sufficiently ingenious as to fool even the advanced collector. Upon close examination, it may be found that a prize plane is nothing but a reworked rabbet.

The last and most interesting group of homemade planes are those in which Yankee ingenuity created a special tool for a job or an improvement upon the available commercial types.

A few examples of homemade planes are illustrated on the following pages.

COREBOX PLANE

The corebox plane is a pattern makers tool used to cut a large semi-circular groove. The plane is actually used to make the final cuts after the center section of the proposed groove is hogged out with a gouge or a gutter plane. The wooden corebox planes noted in collections are all homemade. It is probable that they are handmade versions of the metal planes which Stanley started to produce in 1896. The illustrated plane is an excellent example of the type.

MATCH PLANES

This pair of match planes utilize the same type of handscrew adjustment as used in the familiar wooden clamps. They are also unique in that they are made of hickory. Hickory was seldom used for plane making because of its tendency to split and warp.

COACHMAKERS' PLANES

The coachmakers' planes shown in the illustration are examples of the general type. Inasmuch as they were all homemade, each is a unique item.

MINIATURES

There are many miniature homemade planes which are capable of working wood. These are considered to be in a completely different category than the small unmarked toy planes mentioned under a Special Purpose listing. Two examples of this type of miniatures are shown in the illustration. The small rabbet is about 3½ inches long. The larger plane is 5½ inches long and came from the work bench of a violin maker.

D ROUTER

Wooden routers made in the form of a D are fairly common in America and all appear to be homemade. They are generally 9 to 10 inches in width but wide variations in size have been noted.

WITCHET

The witchet or rounding plane was made commercially in Europe but has not been noted in any list published by American makers. This tool was used for making handles, spokes and similar small cylinders.

DOWELING BOX

The doweling box or dowel cutter is a scarce variety of plane-like tool. The illustrated item has curved cutting irons mounted in non-adjustable positions. Two holes of different sizes are provided in this particular tool. Similar tools may have several holes of different sizes or may have only one hole.

Restoring a Wooden Plane

Most old wooden planes are so covered with an accumulation of dirt and foreign material that a thorough cleaning and refinishing is necessary to restore them to workman-like condition. The original finish was generally a light coat of oil which was quickly lost through either use or neglect. Those items which were originally varnished are even more apt to be mottled because the varnish was generally worn away only in spots. If the particular piece is not excessively dirty or has most of the original varnish intact, wiping with a damp cloth may be all the cleaning that is required.

Most American beechwood is essentially white and turns a light golden tan with age and perspiration. This color cannot be accurately duplicated, therefore replacement of parts should be avoided where at all possible.

The following procedure can be used to restore most any wooden plane to tool-box condition:

1. Disassemble completely. A stubborn wedge can be removed by gripping it in a wood-faced clamp and than tapping the clamp with a hammer.

2. Apply white glue in excess to all cracks and splits and clamp securely. Wipe off excess glue and let set for two hours minimum.

3. Use sandapaper sparingly to trim off ragged edges as necessary to avoid splinters when in use. Trim the top of the wedge with sandpaper if hammer blows have caused the wood to fray or over-run. Do not use sandpaper on the flat surfaces.

All glueing and repair should be completed before application of varnish remover.

4. Apply a commercial paint and varnish remover to all wood parts. Make sure all parts are covered with a thick coating.

5. Straighten the iron with a flat-faced hammer. This step applies mainly to moulding plane irons that are apt to be bent at the soft end.

6. Remove rust and dirt from the iron with a high-speed wire wheel. An eight inch medium wheel mounted on a drill press or grinder spindle does an excellent job. Too much pressure will remove the dark metal coating and impart an unnatural bright finish to the article.

An alternate cleaning method is to soak the metal for 24 hours in a 1/3 solution mixture of vinegar and water and then wipe away the rust with steel wool. Any brass parts should be soaked also if they are badly corroded.

7. By the time the iron has been cleaned with a wire wheel, the varnish remover has done its softening job. Scrape the wood parts with a putty knife to remove the thickest accumulations. Don't be very particular at this stage. Wipe off any excess that will come off on a waste cloth.

8. Proceed immediately to scour each surface with medium steel wool dipped in varnish remover. Keep the steel wool so wet that any loose residue will float in the excess remover. As scouring of each surface is completed, wipe clean with a waste cloth before it has a chance to dry. Additional care

on the toe is sometimes necessary to avoid damage to a weak makers mark. A well struck mark will not be damaged by vigorous application of wet steel wool.

9. Use a dull knife to scrape any remaining dark spots.

10. Rub briskly with clean dry steel wool. This will remove the remaining varnish remover and provide a smooth surface to the wood.

11. If the wood is excessively mottled at this point, a thin application of honey maple stain will usually help to restore an even appearance.

12. Apply a very thin coat of clear varnish, lacquer or sealer. Applying the finish with a soft cloth will provide a coating without the appearance of the tool having been refinished. A special tool such as a fancy panel plow could be given an extra luster with a few coats of gun-stock oil in place of the varnish.

13. Grind and hone the iron.

14. Reassemble the tool and don't forget to let the finish dry adequately before inserting the wedge.

15. Try out the plane on a piece of white pine and adjust the iron for a smooth cut. A piece of shaving left in the throat will provide evidence that you now have a working-quality tool.

A few don'ts are equally important to remember:

1. Don't destroy the makers mark.

2. Don't sand the surface.

3. Don't use oil finish on beechwood. Heavy oil or repeated application of oil will turn the wood increasingly dark.

4. Don't overclean the iron.

5. Don't use a thick coat of varnish on common working tools.

6. Don't use varnish on the irons.

Makers Type Numbers

Some of the larger manufacturers of wooden planes adopted the practice of stamping a number on the toe or heel of the plane. Several of the smaller makers followed suit and numbered their planes using the numbering scheme of one of the larger firms. The numbers are valuable to the collector because they provide positive identification upon comparison of a given plane with the catalogue. Some discretion is necessary in that the numbers were apparently changed somewhat from year to year as various planes were dropped from the listings.

Makers' numbers for three of the larger firms are provided on the following sheets.

REFERENCE NUMBER	NAME	TYPE NUMBER		
		OHIO TOOL CO.	SANDUSKY TOOL CO.	GREENFIELD TOOL CO.
1A1	Smooth Plane	1, 1½, 2, 2¼, 2¾, 3, 3½, 4, 4½, 6, 7¼, 8, 9, 11z, 700	1, 3, 6, 7, 8, 28, 32	5, 12, 23, 31, 38, 44, 50, 56, 62, 66, 70, 76, 90, 91, 92, 93, 96½
1A2	Smooth Plane, Solid Handle	5, 5¼, 7, 7½, 10, 11	4, 5, 5¼, 9, 29	94, 95, 96, 97, 97½, 98, 98½, 99
1A3	Smooth Plane, Jack Handle	5½	5½	99½
1A4	Smooth Plane, German Pattern	2g, 11g		121½, 122½
1A5	Smooth Plane, Front Knob	280, 281, 300, 301, 302		
1A6	Smooth Plane, Handled, Front Knob	304, 305, 306		
1A7	Smooth Plane, Double Razee	282, 283		
1A8	Smooth Plane, Carriage Maker's	11¼	4	
1A9	Smooth Plane, Ship	11S		82, 86
1B1	Jack Plane	12, 12½, 13, 13¼, 14½, 15, 15½, 16, 16½, 17z, 17¼ 702	10, 11, 13, 14, 29, 30, 33	6, 13, 24, 32, 39, 45, 51, 57, 63, 67, 71, 77
1B2	Jack Plane, Razee	14, 17	12, 15	24½, 32½
1B3	Jack Plane, German Pattern	14g, 17g		
1B4	Jack Plane, Double Razee	284		
1B5	Jack Plane, Front Knob	308, 309		
1B6	Jack Plane, Ship	17S		83, 87

REFERENCE NUMBER	NAME	TYPE NUMBER		
		OHIO TOOL CO.	SANDUSKY TOOL CO.	GREENFIELD TOOL CO.
1C1	Fore Plane	18, 18½, 19, 19¼, 20½, 21, 21½, 22, 22½, 23z, 23¼, 704	16, 17, 19 20, 30, 31 34	7, 8, 14, 15, 25, 26, 27, 33, 34, 40, 46, 52, 58, 64, 68 72, 78
1C2	Fore Plane, Razee	20, 23	18, 21	26½, 34½
1C3	Fore Plane, Double Razee	286		
1C4	Fore Plane, Front Knob	311, 312		
1C5	Fore Plane, Ship	235		84, 88
1D1	Jointer Plane	24, 24½, 24¾, 25, 26¼, 27, 27½, 28, 28½, 29z, 706, 708, 710	22, 23, 25, 26, 31, 32, 35	9, 10, 11, 16, 17, 18, 28, 29, 30, 35, 36, 37, 41, 42, 43, 47, 48, 49, 53, 54, 55, 59, 60, 61, 65, 69, 73, 74, 75, 79, 80, 81
1D2	Jointer Plane, Razee	26, 29	24, 27	28½, 29½, 30½, 35½, 36½, 37½
1D3	Jointer Plane, Double Razee	288, 290		
1D4	Jointer Plane, Front Knob	314, 315, 317, 318, 320, 321		
1D5	Jointer Plane, Ship	29S		85, 89
2A1	Mitre Plane, Oval	31, 31¼	38½, 39	110, 111
2A2	Mitre Plane, Square	31¾, 31a	38	110

REFERENCE NUMBER	NAME	TYPE NUMBER		
		OHIO TOOL CO.	SANDUSKY TOOL CO.	GREENFIELD TOOL CO.
2B1	Circular Plane	34, 35	44, 45	116, 117
2C1	Toothing Plane	30, 30¼	36, 36½, 37	109
3A1	Sash Plane, One Iron	125	155	689, 690, 691
3A2	Sash Plane, Two Irons	126, 127	156, 157	692, 693, 694, 712, 713, 714, 715
3A3	Sash Plane, Two Irons, Handled			
3A4	Sash Plane, Screw Arm	128, 129, 130, 131, 131½, 132, 132½, 133	164, 165, 166, 167, 168, 169	701, 702, 703, 704, 705, 706, 707, 708
3A5	Sash Plane, Screw Arm, Handled			716, 717, 718, 719, 720, 721, 794
3A6	Sash Plane, Thumb Screw	133¼, 133½, 134, 134½, 135, 135¼	170, 171, 172, 173	
3A7	Sash Plane, Diamond Pad			698, 699, 700
3B1	Nosing Plane, One Iron	90	111	435½, 436½
3B3	Nosing Plane, One Iron, Applied Handle	90½	112	437
3B4	Nosing Plane, Two Irons	91	113	438½, 439, 439½
3B5	Nosing Plane, Two Irons, Handled	92	114	440
3C1	Table Planes	136, 137	175, 176	733, 735, 737, 738
3C2	Table Planes with Fence	138, 138a	177	734, 735
3D2	Raising Plane, Side Stop	114	144	

REFERENCE NUMBER	NAME	TYPE NUMBER		
		OHIO TOOL CO.	SANDUSKY TOOL CO.	GREENFIELD TOOL CO.
3D4	Raising Jack Plane	115	145	493, 494
3D5	Raising Plane, Screw Arm	32½	42	
3E1	Pump Plane	33	43	119, 120
3E2	Pump Plane, Handled	32	41	118
3F1	Gutter Plane	45¼		209
3G1	Coping Plane	45, 45½	56, 57	208
3G2	Coping Plane, Double	31½		
3H1	Spar Plane	139		731, 732
3K1	Washboard Plane		178	
3L1	Handrail Planes			107
3M1	Toy Planes	2C		100, 101
3M2	Toy Planes	14C		102, 103
3R1	Door Plane, Single	139a	179, 180, 181	270, 271
3R3	Door Plane, Screw Arm	139¼, 139½, 139¾		
3T1	Meeting Rail Plane	135½	174½	
4A1	Rabbet Plane, Skew	116, 117	146, 147	597 thru 644
4A2	Rabbet Plane, Square	120, 121	150, 151	561 thru 596
4A3	Rabbet Plane, Handled	118, 119	148, 149	645 thru 662
4A4	Rabbet Plane, Offset Handle	119½		
4A8	Rabbet Plane, Carriage Makers'	35¾		
4A11	Rabbet Plane, Bridge Builders'			662½
4B1	Filletster	51, 52	65, 66	272, 273, 274

REFERENCE NUMBER	NAME	TYPE NUMBER		
		OHIO TOOL CO.	SANDUSKY TOOL CO.	GREENFIELD TOOL CO.
4B2	Filletster, Side Stop	53, 53½, 54	67, 68	275, 276, 277, 278
4B3	Filletster, Screw Stop	55, 56	69, 70	279, 280, 281, 282, 283
4B4	Filletster, Handled	56½		287, 288, 289, 290, 291, 295, 296
4B6	Filletster, Screw Arm	57	71	284, 285, 286
4B7	Filletster, Screw Arm, Handled	58	72	301 thru 310
4C1	Side Rabbet	123	151½	730
4D1	Halving Plane	68, 69	88, 89	351, 352
4D2	Halving Plane, Handled	70, 71	90, 91	353, 354
5A1	Panel Plow, Screw Arm	95, 96, 98, 99, 102, 103, 106, 107, 107d, 107e	117, 118, 121, 122, 126, 127, 130, 131, 134, 135, 138, 139	509 thru 525
5A2	Panel Plow, Handled	96½, 97, 100, 101, 104, 105, 107a, 107b, 107c, 108, 109	119, 120, 123, 124, 125, 128, 129, 132, 133, 136, 137, 140, 141, 142, 143	526 thru 553
5A3	Panel Plow, Wood Stop	94, 94½	116	503 thru 508
5A4	Panel Plow, Wedge Arms			497, 498, 499
5A5	Panel Plow, Set Screw Arm			500, 501, 502
5B1	Dado, Side Stop	47	60	252
5B2	Dado, Screw Stop	48	62	259

221

REFERENCE NUMBER	NAME	TYPE NUMBER		
		OHIO TOOL CO.	SANDUSKY TOOL CO.	GREENFIELD TOOL CO.
5B3	Dado, Wood Stop		59	245
5C1	Match Planes	75, 75¼, 75½, 76, 76¼, 76½	99, 99½, 100, 100½	382, 383
5C2	Match Planes, Handled	77, 77½, 78, 78½	100, 102	396, 397
5C3	Match Planes, Moving Fence	79, 80, 81	103, 104, 105	410, 411
5C4	Match Planes, Plank			406, 407
5C5	Match Planes, Combination			420, 421
5C8	Match Planes, Screw Arm	82, 83, 84, 84½, 85	106, 107, 108, 109	414, 415, 416, 417, 418, 419
5C9	Match Planes, Wedge Arm			412, 413
6A1	Hollow and Round Pair	72, 73	92, 94	355, 367, 373
6A2	Hollow and Round Pair, Skew	72½, 73½	93, 95	
6B1	Quarter Round	43½	54	555½, 556½, 557½, 558½
6B2	Casing Moulding	43¼		
6B3	Casing Moulding with Fence	43⅛	54¾	
6C1	Cove	43	53	210, 215, 217
6D1	Side Bead	37, 38, 39	47, 48, 49	147 thru 191
6D2	Astragal	36	46	139, 146
6D3	Torus Bead	42½	51½, 52½	740, 741, 742, 743, 744
6E1	Center Bead	41, 42	51, 52	230, 234, 236
6E2	Cock Bead			224, 225
6F1	Reeding Plane	122	152	675, 677, 679,

REFERENCE NUMBER	NAME	TYPE NUMBER		
		OHIO TOOL CO.	SANDUSKY TOOL CO.	GREENFIELD TOOL CO.
6F2	Reeding Plane - 3, 4 or 5 bead	122		
6G1	Snipe Bill	124, 124½	153, 154	728, 729
7A1	Ogee	59	74	444
7B1	Grecian Ogee	60	77	444 thru 454
7B2	Grecian Ogee with Bevel	40, 61¼	79	455 thru 466
7B3	Grecian Ogee with Bead	61½	78	467 thru 477
7B4	Grecian Ogee with Fillet	61	79	
7B6	Grecian Ogee with Quirk & Bead	62¾	75	
7C1	Roman Ogee	59½	76	
7E1	Reverse Ogee	62	81	682 thru 688
7E6	Reverse Ogee with Square	140	96	
7E10	Pilaster	151	98	
7E12	Cabinet Ogee	49	63	201
7F1	Roman Reverse Ogee	62½	82	
7F2	Roman Reverse Ogee with Fence	62¼	82½	
7G1	Grecian Ovolo	63	83	320 thru 326
7G2	Grecian Ovolo with Bevel	65½	84	335 thru 345
7G3	Grecian Ovolo with Bead	65	85	346 thru 350
7G7	Grecian Ovolo with Fillet	64		321 thru 334

223

REFERENCE NUMBER	NAME	TYPE NUMBER		
		OHIO TOOL CO.	SANDUSKY TOOL CO.	GREENFIELD TOOL CO.
7J1	Gothic Bead	66	86	311, 314, 316, 317, 318, 319
7K1	Cove with Bead	44		
7L1	Door Moulding	141	97	
7M1	P. G. Moulding	$43\frac{3}{8}$		
7N1	Nosing Moulding	89	110	434, $434\frac{1}{2}$, 435

224

References

1 Ohio Tool Company, Columbus, Ohio and Auburn, N.Y. Illustrated Price List, 1901

2 The A. J. Harwi Hardware Company, Atchison, Kansas, Catalog No. 67, 1917

3 Roberts, Kenneth O. and Jane W., Planemakers and Other Edge Tool Enterprises in New York State in the Nineteenth Century, New York State Historial Association, Early American Industries Association, 1971

4 The Morton - Simmons Hardware Company, Wichita, Kansas. Morton-Simmons Hardware Encyclopedia, 1908

5 Ohio Tool Company, Charleston, W. Va. Catalogue No. 25, 1914

6 Charles A. Stelinger & Co., Detroit, Michigan. Catalog, Woodworking Tools, 1897

7 John J. Bowles, Hartford, Conn. Price List of Joiners Tools, 1838-1842 (Reprint)

8 J. B. Shannon, Philadelphia, Penn'a Illustrated Catalogue and Price List of Carpenter's Tools, 1873 (Reprint)

9 Mack & Company, Rochester, N.Y. Price list of Genuine "D.R. Barton" Planes, Edge Tools & c. 1877 (Reprint)

10 Sears, Roebuck & Company, Chicago, Illinois. Consumers Guide Catalogue, 1897 (Reprint)

11 Pratt & Company, Buffalo, N.Y. Illustrated Catalogue, 1861. Reprinted in part in Reference 3

12 Huntington, Hopkins & Company, Sacramento and San Francisco, Calif. Hardware Catalogue, 1879

13 Arrowmammett Works, Middletown, Conn. Illustrated Supplement to the Catalogue of Bench Plane, Moulding Tools & c. 1857

14 Arrowmammett Works, Middletown, Conn. Catalog and Invoice Price List of Bench Planes and Moulding Tools. 1858

15 T. B. Rayle & Co., Catalogue Woodworking Tools, Detroit, Mich. 1880s (Reprint)

16 John Denison, Broadside of Joiner's Planes, Winthrop, Conn. 1845-1855 (Reprint)

17 Hermon Chapin, Catalogue and Invoice Prices, Rules, Planes, Gauges & c. Union Factory, Pine Meadows, Conn., 1853 (Reprint)

18 Greenfield Tool Company, Catalogue and Invoice Price List of Joiner's Bench Planes, Moulding Tools, Handles, Plane Irons, & c. Greenfield, Mass. 1872

19 Sargent & Co. Hardware Catalog, New York and New Haven, Conn. 1888

20 Sargent & Company, Hardware Catalogue. 1877

21 The Chapin-Stevens Company, General Catalogue, Union Factory, Pine Meadows, Conn. Subsequent to 1901

22 Simmons Hardware Company Catalogue, St. Louis, Mo. 1880

23 Carpenters and Builders Guide, Volume 1, Theo Audel & Company, 1945

24 The Chronicle of The Early American Industries Association, A Quarterly Publication. Old Economy, Ambridge, Pennsylvania

25 Sears, Roebuck & Company, Chicago, Illinois. Blacksmith Tools and Supplies Catalogue. 1900

26 Knight, Edward H., Knight's American Mechanical Dictionary, 3 volumes, Houghten, Mufflen and Company, 1882

27 Every Man His Own Mechanic, Rohde and Haskins, New York and London. 1900

28 Brown, William, The Carpenter's Assistant, Livermore & Rudd, New York. 1856

29 The Sandusky Tool Company, Catalogue of Tools, Sandusky Ohio. 1877

30 Alexander-Yost Co., Catalogue No. 3, Cooper's Tools and Supplies, San Francisco, Calif. 1906

31 The Sandusky Tool Company, Catalogue of Tools, Sandusky, Ohio. 1885

32 A. F. Brombacher & Co., Inc., Catalogue of Tools for Coopers and Gaugers. 1922 (Reprint)

33 V.A. Emond and Co. Catalogue of Bench, Moulding and Coopers Planes. 1889

34 Sem. Dalpé, Catalogue of Carpenters Planes, Roxton Pond, Quebec. 1889

35 Hasluck, Paul N., The Handyman's Book, Cassell & Co., Ltd., London. 1905

36 Salaman, R.A., Dictionary of Tools, Charles Scribner & Co., New York, 1975

37 Roberts, Kenneth D., Wooden Planes in 19th Century America, Fitzwilliam, N.H. 1975

39 Hyson's Tool and Supply Company, St. Louis, Mo. Catalog of Coopers Tools. 1902

40 F.K. Collins, Ravenna, Ohio, List of Joiners' Tools. 1838

41 The L. & I.J. White Company, Buffalo, N.Y. Catalogue of Coopers' Tools including Turpentine Tools. 1912 (reprint)

42 Martin, Richard A., The Wooden Plane, Early American Industries Association, 1977

Index

Grecian ovolo with raised square, 177
Grecian ovolo with square, 177
Grecian ovolo with torus bead, 177
Grecian reverse ogee, 166
Grooving planes, 105
Gutter plane, 70

Halving plane, 103
Halving plane, handled, 104
Handrail planes, 75
Head cutter, 203
Head float, 202
Head float, Cleveland pattern, 203
Heading float, 202
Heald patent smooth plane, 25
Heel plane, 42
Hodgman's pattern leveling plane, 193
Hollow and round pair, 131
Hollow and round pair, skew, 133
Homemade planes, 207
Horn scrub plane, 45
Horn smooth plane, 22
Howel, 191
Howel and croze combination, 204
Howel, beer, 195
Howel, gouge, 194
Howel, shifting, 195
Howel, stock, 194
Howel, tight barrel, 194

Intermediate smooth plane, 17
Iron block croze, 199

Jack plane, 28, 29
Jack plane, double razee, 31
Jack plane, front knob, 31
Jack plane, German pattern, 30
Jack plane, razee, 29
Jack plane, ship, 32
Jack rabbet, 89
Jarvis, carriage makers', 84
Jointer, coopers', 191
Jointer, long, 36
Jointer, picture frame, 42
Jointer plane, 36
Jointer plane, double razee, 37
Jointer plane, front knob, 37
Jointer plane, lightweight, 38

Jointer plane, razee, 37
Jointer plane, ship, 38
Jointer, short, 33

Lambs tongue, 165
Lance croze, 196
Leveler, 193
Leveller, 193
Leveling and croze combination, 205
Leveling and howel combination, 204
Leveling plane, 193
Leveling plane, keg, 193
Lightweight jointer, 38
Long jointer, 36
Long plane, 17
Long rabbet plane, 93

Match planes, 116
Match plane, combination, 120
Match plane, combination, handled, 121
Match plane, double, 120
Match planes, moving, 122
Match planes, moving fence, 118
Match planes, plank, 119
Match planes, screw arm, 122
Match plane, twin, 120
Match plane, wedge arm, 123
Meeting rail plane, 83
Miniature planes, 211
Mitre plane, oval, 40
Mitre plane, picture frame, 42
Mitre plane, square, 41
Mitre plane, Worrall patent, 41
Moulding planes, 126
Moving match planes, 122
Moving sash, diamond pad, 57

New Jersey shifting croze, 199
Nosing bilection, 183
Nosing moulding, 183
Nosing planes, 59
Nosing lane, center throat, 62
Nosing plane, 1 iron, 60
Nosing plane, 1 iron, applied handle, 61
Nosing plane, 1 iron, solid handle, 60
Nosing plane, 2 irons, 61
Nosing plane, 2 irons, handled, 62
Nosing step plane, 60